Beyond Rhetoric

Beyond Rhetoric

Reconciliation as a Way of Life

SAMUEL GEORGE HINES
and
CURTISS PAUL DEYOUNG

with Dalineta L. Hines

Foreword by Cheryl J. Sanders
Special Introduction by Dalineta L. Hines

Judson Press
Valley Forge

Library of Congress Cataloging-in-Publication Data

Hines, Samuel G.
    Beyond rhetoric : reconciliation as a way of life / Samuel George Hines and Curtiss Paul DeYoung ; foreword by Cheryl J. Sanders ; special introduction by Dalineta L. Hines.
        p.   cm.
    ISBN 0-8170-1329-6 (pbk. : alk. paper)
    1. Reconciliation—Religious aspects—Christianity.   I. DeYoung, Curtiss Paul.
II. Title.
BT738.28 H56   2000
234′.5—dc21   99-047260

Printed in the U.S.A.

06 05 04 03 02 01 00

10 9 8 7 6 5 4 3 2

In memory of Samuel G. Hines

late husband of Dalineta, with whom she shared
forty-one and one-half years of a uniquely blessed marriage
and a broad spectrum of pastoral and reconciling ministries.

In memory of the late John H. Staggers Jr.

one of Samuel Hines' covenant brothers who shared with us
the vision of reconciliation of all people everywhere,
to God and to each other.

In honor of Dalineta L. Hines

a tireless ambassador of reconciliation and
a mother in the faith to Curtiss DeYoung and many others.

In honor of Karen Maria DeYoung

the much beloved wife of Curtiss DeYoung and
an inspiring example of authentic reconciliation lived out every day.

CONTENTS

FOREWORD

I OFFER THIS FOREWORD TO *BEYOND RHETORIC* FROM THREE DISTINCT vantage points—first, as a member of Third Street Church of God in Washington, D.C., during Dr. Samuel Hines' twenty-five-year tenure as senior pastor; second, as his successor, charged with the responsibility of leading a congregation that yet bears marks of his influence and of the impact of his convictions; and third, as a Christian ethicist with a concern for observing and understanding how the principle of reconciliation actually plays out in church and society.

From the time of his installation as pastor of the Third Street Church of God on Sunday, September 7, 1969, Dr. Hines set as his pastoral priority the care of souls. His idea of worship was to offer praise and prayers to God with dignity, sincerity, and reverence. He wrote eloquent papers for our edification each year, whose content is represented in the pages that follow. But the hallmark of his pastoral ministry was his total dedication to excellent preaching. Week after week, he prepared thoroughly with comprehensive study, creative exegesis of the Scripture, and careful choice of words to communicate effectively his deepest insights into God's Word. Every Sunday his sermon would bring a confirmation or affirmation or challenge directly to our lives. Whether at prayer meeting, pastoral staff meeting, church council meeting, or wherever else we gathered to do the Lord's work, Dr. Hines was ready with a word from God or a meditation drawn from the depths of his own daily spiritual disciplines. His learning reached far beyond his academic degrees, and he was an encyclopedic resource on anything having to do with the church and ministry.

Reconciliation was unquestionably the central theme undergirding the pastoral ministry of Dr. Hines. He continually challenged the congregation to become "Ambassadors for Christ in the Nation's Capital" and to embody the message of reconciliation articulated by the apostle Paul in 2 Corinthians 5:17–21. He insisted that the weight of biblical evidence places great responsibilities on the church to minister to the poor. Under his leadership, the congregation's energies and resources became focused on bringing the powerful and powerless together in ministry among the urban poor, guided by his conviction that "dogma divides and mission unites." Early on Dr. Hines invested his time and energies in community involvement by working with numerous government agencies, community organizations, and ecumenical groups.

I was invited by Dr. Hines to serve on the pastoral staff as associate pastor for leadership development in 1985, and I remained in that position until I was called by the congregation to become senior pastor in 1997. During the 1980s I came to know Curtiss DeYoung, first as an urban ministry intern at Third Street Church of God and later as a colleague and copresenter in the ministry of reconciliation.

Under my leadership, the congregation has sought additional funding and personnel in order to expand the three major programs initially developed by Dr. Hines: (1) the Urban Breakfast, which provides a daily worship experience and morning meal followed by counseling, Bible study, and social services for people who live in the local shelters and on the streets; (2) the weekly distribution of groceries for families and individuals in the community; and (3) the U.N.I.Q.U.E. Learning Center, a tutorial and counseling program that meets daily throughout the year to provide educational support and counseling to thirty or more community children.

The ministry partnership between Third Street Church of God and the National Presbyterian Church in Washington, D.C., remains a vital component of our vision of reconciliation. A core group of volunteers from that congregation continue to present their gifts and resources on a regular basis, and we share in ongoing dialogue with pastors Craig Barnes, Lynne Faris, and others around the issues of poverty and race. A new initiative, actually a new model for reconciliation, is underway in partnership with a suburban Korean Presbyterian congregation to create a ministry organization that will erect a dedicated urban ministry facility to enhance the churches' ability to serve the needs of the community.

I mentioned a third perspective that I bring to bear upon this volume—that of a Christian ethicist. I have taught ethics at the Howard University School of Divinity since 1984, and my special interest has been the interplay between religion and society. My scholarship has borne fruit in the publication of five books, including *How Firm a Foundation* (1990), a history of the Third Street Church of God, and *Saints in Exile* (1996), a study of ethics and worship in the Holiness-Pentecostal tradition. It was my privilege to observe, close at hand, the life and work of a man whose devotion to the idea of reconciliation was as profound as his praxis. For this reason, Third Street Church of God has been for me an ideal context for testing ideas and insights pertaining to the empowerment of the urban poor. A careful reading of the present volume will help to move the reconciliation dialogue in this nation beyond rhetoric to the place where more of us, in the church and in the society, can acquire an informed understanding of what reconciliation is in light of the Scriptures; a keen sense of what reconciliation brings to the practice of ministry; and a foretaste of the healing and hope that reconciliation promises for a hostile and divided world.

Cheryl J. Sanders
Washington, D.C.
August 1999

ACKNOWLEDGMENTS

I WISH TO SAY A WORD OF DEEP AND APPRECIATIVE THANKFULNESS TO GOD for sparing my life and to my four wonderful children—David, Milton, Charmaine, and Delmarie—who stood by me in the shocking grief of my husband's, their father's, sudden death. They then joined hands and hearts to nurse me back from unexpected coronary bypass surgery and gave quality assistance in creating this book. I love you all forever.

My heartfelt thanks to Curtiss Paul DeYoung—a "son in the gospel"—for his insightful contributions to this volume, his skillful editing, and his unfailing encouragement.

Special words of appreciation to Jewel Cripe for her help in outlining the "Pew to Pavement" section and also to Steve Gibson for his splendid graphic art input.

Dalineta L. Hines

I first must thank Dalineta L. Hines for trusting me with her husband's treasured manuscripts. I feel highly honored. Mrs. Hines and I offer a word of gratitude to the staff at Judson Press for their help and commitment to this project. We also express our deepest appreciation to Cheryl Sanders for writing the foreword to this book. Her life is a living tribute to the message contained herein.

Words of appreciation go to Deb (Carter) Michlin, Sabrena Hildreth, and Mercy Olson-Ward for typing portions of this manuscript. Thanks also to the TURN staff and board of directors for their constant support. I express my sincere gratitude to three individuals who read the manuscript and offered important insights that strengthened this book significantly: William Huff for his constant affirmation, Claudia May for her faithfulness in prayer and commitment to excellence, and Aldean Miles for his endless encouragement and abundant praise.

This book celebrates my father-son ministry partnership with Samuel Hines. I have been richly blessed with many fathers and mothers in my life. Without the significant influence of my own parents, I would not be where I am today. My first and foremost father in ministry, Rev. Arnold DeYoung, exemplified for me the importance of integrity. My mother, Marylin (Curtiss) DeYoung, showed me that one does not need ordination to serve God in ministry. I gained two more wonderful parents through marriage—Hoover and Vivian McBee. I must also give honor to two other fathers in ministry—Levorn Aaron and James Earl Massey.

I express much love and gratitude to my wife, Karen, for supporting me in this project. She loved Sam Hines as much as I did. I am grateful for the wonderful encouragement I received from my children, Rachel and Jonathan. My hope for the future resides in the God who reconciled us through Jesus Christ!

Curtiss Paul DeYoung

INTRODUCTIONS

A Unique Book

CURTISS PAUL DEYOUNG

A FEW YEARS AGO, SINGER NATALIE COLE RECORDED A DUET OF THE SONG "Unforgettable" with her father, Nat King Cole. It was one of her father's best-known songs. What made the song unique was that through the magic of modern technology she recorded this duet with her father after he died. (Even a music video of their duet was produced.) The way their voices blended on the recording made the duet even more compelling. You could hear traces of the master singer Nat King Cole's phrasing and vocal prowess in his daughter's singing. One could easily determine where Natalie had learned to sing. Yet Natalie made contributions to the song that belonged uniquely to her. She had learned much from her father, but she also had grown to the point in her development where she could freely add her own nuances to the song. In a sense, she put her own signature on it. The resulting duet was truly unforgettable.

This book is a unique father-and-son duet. The late Reverend Doctor Samuel George Hines was my father in the ministry. Pastor Hines (as many of us called him) mentored me as a member of his staff at Third Street Church of God in Washington, D.C., officiated at my wedding to Karen, laid hands on me in ordination, and counseled me regarding major decisions in my life. He also modeled for me what it means to be a servant leader, a minister of the gospel, and an ambassador of reconciliation. I still deeply miss him since his sudden death on January 6,

1995. When his widow, Dalineta L. Hines, brought me the manuscript of what is contained in this book, I felt excited to once again hear the master expositor "sing" his best-known song—*reconciliation*. As his words jumped off the page, engaging my mind and spirit, I discovered to my amazement how much of what I preach, teach, and write about reconciliation took shape through my relationship with Samuel Hines.

Hines was perhaps best known for his reconciliation ministry concerning issues of race, class, and poverty. Particularly noteworthy was how "he gave critical behind-the-scenes leadership to the demolition of apartheid in South Africa by aggressive and focused counseling of church leaders, political activists, and governmental leaders."[1] He proved equally effective at home. As an urban ministry intern at Third Street Church of God in Washington, D.C., during Hines' pastorate, I listened as members described the impact of his expository preaching on the subject of reconciliation. I remember being told by one member that she had hated white people, yet she could not withstand the persuasive power of the Holy Spirit speaking through Dr. Hines' sermons on reconciliation.

Rev. Hines' commitment to reconciliation across class and economic lines emerged early in his life. He was born in Savanna-la-mar, Westmoreland, on the isle of Jamaica. His father was a pioneer Church of God pastor on that island, and his Jamaican mother was a graduate of Tuskegee Institute. The Hines' home was a place where faith was exercised every day. This was due in part to their poverty because of the limited financial support pastors received. As Samuel Hines said, "It used to take at least three miracles a day to keep us alive: one for breakfast, one for lunch, and one for dinner. And they all took place on a daily basis."[2] In the midst of their own poverty and need, Sam Hines observed his father reach out through his ministry to others who faced similar challenges.

During the fifty years of Samuel Hines' ministry, he reached out to many people who struggled in life. Evidence of this could be found at the daily Urban Prayer Breakfast held at Third Street Church of God, where, as the present pastor of that church, Cheryl Sanders, writes, "Hines emphasized reconciliation across class and racial lines so that the hospitality of a hot meal and a warm welcome could be extended to refugees of the urban crisis—the homeless, prostitutes, drug addicts, and the unemployed."[3] Every day several hundred people gathered to partake of food for the stomach and nourishment for the soul followed by insightful counseling in every area that affects human life. Samuel Hines demonstrated God's love to those gathered through his powerful preaching, wise counsel, warm embrace, and hearty laugh.[4] The impact of Dr. Hines' ministry can still be felt among formerly homeless individuals from the streets of Washington, D.C., through all social strata, including leaders on Capitol Hill. It still reverberates throughout the United States and in Jamaica, South Africa, Germany, Kenya, and elsewhere.

As you read this book, you will discover that Samuel Hines addressed reconciliation from a much broader perspective than race and class. He lived a commitment to reconciliation that reached into every aspect of his life and the lives of those who came in contact with him. Samuel Hines was an artisan of reconciliation. James Earl Massey, a noted preacher and practitioner of reconciliation in his own right, has written that Hines "was one of this century's ablest exponents of the reconciliation theme, and he was a primary example of how to engage in the ministry of reconciling."[5] Dr. Hines steadfastly pursued his passion of following Jesus Christ in the ministry of reconciliation. Many of us thank God for Samuel George Hines—a priceless treasure enjoyed by the church around the world. This book, *Beyond Rhetoric: Reconciliation as a Way of Life,* provides an opportunity for you to be challenged, and hopefully changed, as a result of interacting with the profound, yet very practical, message of holistic reconciliation delivered by Sam Hines.

This book is also a duet. I blend the message of reconciliation as God has called me to expound it with that of Dr. Hines' voice. I contribute chapters that merge amazingly well with what is offered by my father in ministry. I use anecdotes from his life and comments from his writings to enhance my chapters. Yet my witness to the reconciliation message also offers particular nuances on the subject that have emerged since leaving the direct oversight of Dr. Hines at his laboratory of reconciliation ministry in Washington, D.C.

Along my delightful and demanding pilgrimage, I have offered some reflections on the subject of reconciliation. My first book, *Coming Together: The Bible's Message in an Age of Diversity,* addressed the biblical, theological, cultural, and historical understandings needed for bridging the wide chasm that exists in our world and in the church. *Reconciliation: Our Greatest Challenge, Our Only Hope,* my second book, offered a definition of biblical reconciliation, noted several barriers, and proposed a process for moving forward in reweaving human relationships. The chapters I contribute to this volume contain new material developed since the writing of those books.

Beyond Rhetoric is divided into three major sections. The first section focuses on the biblical theology needed for the ministry of reconciliation. In the second section, our attention turns to the role of the church as an agent of reconciliation. The third and final section addresses the practice of reconciliation. Our hope is to fully engage the reader with this book. Therefore, discussion questions are included at the end of each chapter and a supplemental workbook section at the end of the book offers some practical interactive resources.

We are all deeply indebted to Dalineta Hines for her tireless efforts in preserving her husband's works so that we can benefit from them. She has selected all of his material included in this book, and together we have edited Dr. Hines' contributions. Mrs. Hines has also continued to pursue the ministry of reconciliation that she and Pastor Hines shared for so many years. God is transforming many lives through her faithfulness. I am also thankful to Mrs. Hines for her strong love and support through the years for my family and me. I sincerely hope your soul will be nourished by this duet of a father and son in ministry as we proclaim the timeless message of reconciliation first announced two thousand years ago by Jesus Christ. It is a truly unforgettable word.

NOTES

1. Cheryl J. Sanders, *Saints in Exile: The Holiness-Pentecostal Experience in African American Religion* (Oxford: Oxford University Press, 1996), 40.
2. Samuel Hines, "Nobody with Your Color Eyes Can Be a Preacher," interviewed in William H. Myers, *The Irresistible Urge to Preach: A Collection of African American "Call" Stories* (Atlanta: Aaron Press, 1992), 158.
3. Sanders, *Saints in Exile,* 42.
4. At the writing of this book, Hines' eldest son, David, continues the tradition of his father as he directs the multidimensional aspects of urban ministry that arise from the daily Urban Prayer Breakfast.
5. James Earl Massey, foreword in Samuel G. Hines, *Experience the Power* (Anderson, Ind.: Warner, 1993, 1995), vii.

A Unique Man

DALINETA L. HINES

"THE GIFTS AND CALLING OF GOD ARE WITHOUT REPENTANCE" (ROMANS 11:29, KJV). This truth of God was a guiding principle in the life of Samuel George Hines—a preacher's kid—who, for fifty and one-half years used the gifts and talents with which God had blessed him to bless others. He studied, taught, proclaimed, and modeled a transparently godly lifestyle and exemplary Christlike attitude in all kinds of circumstances as he interacted with all types of people. He was an anointed proclaimer of God's Word, an insightful Bible teacher, a just and compassionate administrator, a gifted pastor, a peerless husband and father and a humble servant-leader.

Multitudes of persons, including his ministerial peers, were inspired and edified by this redeemed child of God. He was totally submitted to the Holy Spirit, indefatigable in his study of God's Word, intensely faithful in intercessory prayer, unusually knowledgeable about world history, and had a Godly insight into human personality. His formal education, coupled with a lifetime of autodidactic learning in all areas relating to theology, preaching, and every aspect of the human experience, equipped him to be an unparalleled messenger of the Word and work of God.

Reconciliation was a basic theme of his ministry. This unique and relevant book on reconciliation is a distillation of selections from some of the powerful Spirit-anointed messages and teaching seminars he delivered on this subject in his five pastorates, as well as to groups across Washington, D.C., throughout the United States, and around the world.

Sam Hines was one of those few persons who ministered effectively across all religious, racial, cultural, political, generational, and gender boundaries and who gained the respect of the powerful even as he earned the trust of the powerless. He was an astute and effective counselor for troubled and/or seeking individuals and groups at all levels of society.

While doing the final revisions for this manuscript, I came across a complete outline that Sam had written for a book that he had intended to write. It was dated three years before his death! The title of the manuscript was "Reconciliation." Within that outline, he stated his purpose for engaging in such an endeavor:

> I hope that after making clear the theological foundation for godly reconciliation, the text will give people some guidelines that they can follow, from wherever they may be in the spectrum of life, as they seek to practice reconciliation. It must be a book that can be used for practical applications in a variety of broken relationships. Hopefully, it will also help them to prevent relational fracturing. The volume ought also to be useful to local congregations and agencies, by helping them to evaluate their interactions with each other and with persons not of their own persuasions. Above all, it must steer them in the direction of determining whether or not their motivations for ministry are appropriately aligned with the divine agenda.

It is my prayer that both God's purposes and Sam's desires will be met and that the Holy Spirit will use this book to help people everywhere to get a fresh and vital look at the glory of God as well as a clearer perception of the divine plan for holistic reconciliation.

The Theme of My Life

SAMUEL GEORGE HINES

WHEN PREACHERS GET TO A CERTAIN AGE, THEIR PREACHING USUALLY revolves around a theme. They think in these terms when asked to speak anywhere, whether in halls of power, on street corners, or in churches around the world. Very early in my Christian walk the Lord made it clear to me that the number one priority on God's agenda, or work in the world, is *reconciliation*.

Let me give you an early reconciliation episode that creates a background for my life and ministry.[1] I am a preacher's kid. My father served the same church until he died. I lived in a strictly rigid, inflexible, conservative, evangelical household. I was forbidden to do many things; for instance, I could not go to movies. I could not participate in many things most young people do because of the brand of religion to which I was exposed. So I made some plans to get away from home as fast as I could. One of my motivations for doing well in high school was to graduate and get away from the bondage that I felt in my home.

During my last year in high school, something of critical importance happened in my life. A visiting preacher came to Jamaica and conducted meetings in my father's church. He lived in our house during this time. Now I had to cope with two preachers, my dad and this evangelist. I battled with them, verbally, every day of the week. One day the visiting preacher said that he wanted to see the countryside and asked me to go bicycle riding with him. We borrowed two bicycles and rode along the country lanes. He talked religion all the way and bored me to death! He talked about Christ, the Bible, and salvation, subjects that I had heard about all my life. When we got back, I returned the bicycles intact. That night the person from whom we had borrowed the bicycles complained to my father that I had ruined one bicycle. She said that I had purposefully returned it without reporting the damage. My father believed her when she called me a liar and an evil person. Then he punished me for something I had not done.

At that time I had a violent, vicious temper, and I resolved to be avenged on this person. But on the next day, a Sunday, I got saved—born again. This preacher's kid got saved! My heart and my life changed instantaneously. Hatred and bitterness left me completely, and I began loving her and no longer wanted to hurt her. I was almost upset with myself for going through that change. Then I realized that it was for my benefit that it had happened. I am not sure that she ever changed her mind about me, but I changed my mind about her. I am not sure that she was ever reconciled to me, but I was reconciled to her. Some years later I became her pastor. She was a precious person, and I loved her until she died. We both hope to get to glory; and when we get there, we will not discuss that bicycle.

Reconciliation with God and each other through Christ is the number one item on God's agenda. Oneness must be realized in the midst of an environment prone to alienation and polarization. God is not ignorant of the fact that the trends in our society move toward separateness. We called it apartheid in South Africa and condemned it, but we are more generous to our own brands of discrimination here at home. Realistically, reconciliation is not an option either for the Christian or the non-Christian. It is a restoration that creates wholeness in relationships where brokenness, dehumanization and polarization have existed. Reconciliation brings about peace, both between human beings and God and between individual persons. In spite of all the efforts we make to come together, barriers exist and keep driving us apart. God conceived of reconciliation before the formation of the world. Before the foundations of the world were in place, God provided a Lamb, slain ahead of time, for our atonement. What do you get when you break down atonement? AT-ONE-MENT. That has been God's intention from the very beginning. If I want to be in line with God's agenda in my own life, reconciliation must also be my number one priority. Further, it must be the primary agenda of the universal church of God.

> So if anyone is in Christ, there is a new creation: everything old has passed away; see, everything has become new! All this is from God, who reconciled us to himself through Christ, and has given us the ministry of reconciliation; that is, in Christ God was reconciling the world to himself, not counting their trespasses against them, and entrusting the message of reconciliation to us. So we are ambassadors for Christ, since God is making his appeal through us; we entreat you on behalf of Christ, be reconciled to God. For our sake he made him to be sin who knew no sin, so that in him we might become the righteousness of God (2 Corinthians 5:17–21).

NOTE

1. For more biographical details on Samuel Hines and his call to ministry, see William H. Myers' interview with Samuel Hines, "Nobody with Your Color Eyes Can Be a Preacher," in William H. Myers, *The Irresistible Urge to Preach: A Collection of African American "Call Stories"* (Atlanta: Aaron Press, 1992), 157–68.

SECTION I

A Biblical Theology of Reconciliation

First Things First

Thinking Reconciliation Precedes
Doing Reconciliation

SAMUEL GEORGE HINES
(with a response by Curtiss Paul DeYoung)

IN 1978 I RECEIVED AN INVITATION TO SPEAK AT SOME VERY HIGH-LEVEL meetings in South Africa on the radical remedy of reconciliation. After giving my presentation, I began to take my seat when a black minister stood to his feet and said, "Sam Hines, you are late. South Africa cannot tolerate reconciliation right now. We have tried that for a long time. We need revolution. Reconciliation is too soft and namby-pamby. We need something rugged and tough."

That kind of attack pushed my buttons, so I got up and said, "Sir, I will not allow you to define my term and judge me by your definition. Reconciliation is not soft and namby-pamby. It is rugged and tough. Herein lies the difference between the revolutionary and the reconciler. The revolutionary says, 'The world is in trouble, in bad shape; it needs to be fixed, and I am going to work to fix it. If you get in my way, I will kill you, because I must do what I have to do.' The reconciler says, 'The world is in bad shape; it must be changed, and I am going to work to change it. If you confront me and try to block me, I am willing to lay down my life for this cause.'" I then asked, "Which of these positions is soft and namby-pamby?"

There is no softness or cheapness about reconciliation. The reconciler is willing to pay the ultimate price of giving up the right for revenge, even to the extent of laying down his or her life for the cause.

Reconciliation is the way of the cross—love pressing its way even in the face of death. We must take the path our Savior took. Yet before we can faithfully consider the impact of such a choice, we require a time of preparation. We need to embrace a radical new way of thinking. As the saying goes, "First things first." Thinking reconciliation precedes doing reconciliation. We must learn how to comprehend God's thoughts, because the concept of reconciliation does not originate in our minds. Reconciliation is God's idea. Therefore, our thoughts must conform to the mind of God. Until we can think God's thoughts, we will struggle uselessly in our attempts to act as God would act in a given situation. The reconciler recognizes and believes that reconciliation is God's one-item agenda. God is the author of reconciliation. People only carry out the reconciling process that God initiated. Reconciliation begins between God and human beings, through the atonement of Jesus Christ, and then is channeled through us to each other by the empowerment of the Holy Spirit. Many reconciling projects are only of brief duration because the doers cannot think in God's terms. What are God's thoughts? Whenever God thinks about this planet or this universe, the summary and the substance of the Almighty's thinking is reconciliation—oneness. How often is that? As often as always. Reconciliation is always a "today" word and therefore a continuous process.

Radically Changed Relationships

More than emotional reactions, social adjustments, or political maneuverings, reconciliation transcends all humanly motivated efforts to get people together. Biblical reconciliation comes through the atoning work of Jesus Christ on the cross. The word most frequently translated "reconciliation" in the New Testament literally means to change completely, thoroughly, or radically. We can feel the impact of the original word when we read passages like Romans 5:10 and 2 Corinthians 5:18–20 if we substitute the literal meaning wherever "reconciliation" or other related words occur. Let me illustrate this with the two passages I just mentioned. Romans 5:10 reads, "For if while we were enemies, we were reconciled to God through the death of his Son, much more surely, having been reconciled, will we be saved by his life." By replacing "reconciliation" with the literal meaning, it might read, "For if while we were enemies, our relationship to God was *changed completely* through the death of his Son, much more surely, having been *radically transformed,* will we be saved by his life."

Let us also observe how a similar exchange adds to the meaning of the glorious 2 Corinthians text that has inspired so many of us to pursue this ministry. Second Corinthians 5:18–20 states: "All this is from God, who reconciled us to himself through Christ, and has given us the ministry of reconciliation; that is, in Christ God was reconciling the world to himself, not counting their trespasses against them, and entrusting the message of reconciliation to us. So we are ambassadors for Christ, since God is making his appeal through us; we entreat you on behalf of Christ, be reconciled to God." Again by interchanging "reconciliation" with the literal meaning this text could read: "All this is from God, who *thoroughly changed* our relationship to himself through Christ, and has given us the ministry of *radical relational transformation;* that is, in Christ God *completely changed* the world's *relationship* to himself, not counting their trespasses against them, and entrusting the message of this *radical change* to us. So we are ambassadors for Christ, since God is making his appeal through us; we entreat you on behalf of Christ, be *changed completely in your relationship* with God."

In nonbiblical terms, reconciliation means bridging historical and traditional gaps between individuals, stimulating people to have mutual respect for each other and helping them to understand that we are all part of a "oneness" that we violate at our own risk. Biblical reconciliation embraces all of these, but then goes beyond them. The process directs our thinking and perceptions to God's parameters of unbiased love, unconditional forgiveness, humble repentance, and generous reparation, wherever and whenever possible. Godly reconciliation therefore takes us beyond speaking theology to living theologically.

The substitution of the literal meaning for "reconciliation" in these two texts demonstrates more fully the power and impact of this word and ministry. The revelation here is that in the interest of all people, God effected such a provision for radical change, as makes possible a completely new relationship with God and with other persons.

Our stewardship of this word and ministry of reconciliation makes us responsible to proclaim the good news of this provision to all people, irrespective of race, gender, age, nationality, culture, or denomination. Within the reconciled community this radical change affects, not only our relationship with God, but also our relationships with one another.

The apostle Paul became ecstatic in his letter to the church in Ephesus when he wrote about the ultimate divine purpose of cosmic reunification (1:7–2:22). Jesus Christ, the center of the circle of reconciliation and fulcrum of our faith, is the point from which energy flows to all who would become agents of reconciliation. Reconcilers have to "overlive" the malice, hatred, and bitterness of abused and dispossessed persons around them. Under God, reconcilers do not allow other persons to control either their minds or their actions and reactions. This is in order to prevent their becoming disqualified to be God's agents of reconciliation.

Ghetto Tendencies

When we seek to think God's thoughts, we struggle not with God, and not ultimately with others, but with ourselves. We all have to fight the ghetto tendencies within us. We all are prone to box ourselves into limited spaces. Racially, it happens in our society as people force others to live in ghettos so that they may be free to live their own separate existence. Religiously, it happens as we try to build systems around ideas, interpretations of Scripture, and spiritual experiences, so that our uniqueness does not add to the unity in diversity, but rather to the fragmentation of truth. Politically, it happens as parties and individuals strive, not just to make their contribution to the national welfare, but to engineer the destruction of those whose policies are in conflict with their own. The generation and gender gaps are manifestations of the same spirit that limits people by separating them into gulfs of suspicion and alienation.

The somber reality is that even physical ghettos do not just happen. Ghettos are made intentionally. Self-interest, competition, prosperity cults, and hostility toward the poor have left us with inner cities that are becoming or have already become disfigured battlegrounds all across the United States and the world. If we add to this private preferences, political choices, traditional decisions, protective measures, plus the proneness to turn our heads the other way, we sooner or later all face the result of our bad planning or lack of planning. Such a result leaves us miles apart from God's plan of reconciliation. The temptation is to move away from God's divine agenda, find an easier "fix" for ourselves, and substitute some halfhearted efforts of rehabilitation and legal steps toward integration. When the gap widens between deprived people who are left behind and successful people who move forward, the reconciliation agenda becomes more urgent and more pressing in our society. Despite the belief that our cities are overwhelming us, the spiritual reality is that they are being overwhelmed by the nature of Satan.

The Reconciled Community

Reconciliation is love confronting these ghetto tendencies. We, the people of God, must not just tell the world to reconcile. People need to see us together, networking the kingdom of God, on the basis of reconciled relationships. Local congregations and other wider manifestations of the church's witness must confront the world with the living reality of reconciliation. Reconciling action begins as we address the heart of our existence as a fellowship of believers and see unity in community. This is not a call to tokenism or to uniformity. It is a challenge to practice what we preach. Here the promotion of unity becomes the path of humility and self-sacrifice. Practical and practiced love for one another is the badge of faith. As Jesus said, "By this everyone will know that you are my disciples, if you have love for one another" (John 13:35). Prejudice, pride, bigotry, and discrimination do not politely bow to slogans, preachments about the law of love, civil rights legislation, or movement pressure toward integration. Reconciliation calls us to oneness, not sameness.

So how should we *think* reconciliation, before *doing* reconciliation? The godly reconciler promotes and practices reconciliation from a biblical, holistic perspective. As the apostle Paul wrote, "All this is from God, who reconciled us to himself through Christ, and has given us the ministry of reconciliation" (2 Corinthians 5:18). I cannot emphasize this enough; reconciliation brings about the restoration of right relationships between God and humankind and between individuals of both genders, all races, cultures, levels of society, nationalities, and denominational persuasions. Reconciliation goes beyond integration or accommodation because it flows out of repentance and forgiveness—both vertically with God and horizontally with each other. Reconciliation, God's one-item agenda, must become our agenda. God's thoughts must become our thoughts. It is then, and only then, that we can move from *thinking* reconciliation to *doing* reconciliation, because our action will be in sync with God's desired action. Every Christian is given the mandate to become an intentional ambassador of godly, holistic reconciliation.

Response by Curtiss Paul DeYoung

SAMUEL HINES REMINDS US THAT WE MUST ATTEND TO FIRST THINGS first—thinking reconciliation precedes doing reconciliation. Our character must contain more than a residue of God's atoning work in Jesus Christ. Only as we exhibit more and more of the likeness of Jesus Christ can we fully embrace the ministry of reconciliation. Hines declares that the first work of reconciliation is the internal work by God in our own lives. God's love for us produces in us a love for others. This process of being reconciled to God lasts a lifetime. Every day we conform a bit more to the character of Jesus Christ. Each of us is a work in progress. Reconciliation occurs in the midst of daily life—lived in the presence of God. Therefore, the call to ambassadorial status in the ministry of reconciliation requires a daily response.

Since reconciliation embodies a lifestyle rather than merely a strategy for human relations, we must embrace reconciliation as a spiritual discipline—a godly habit. Howard Thurman included reconciliation as one of seven spiritual disciplines in his 1963 book, *Disciplines of the Spirit*. He wrote, "Reconciliation and the harmony that it produces must be experienced by the individual as a normal routine."[1] We must integrate reconciliation into our living in such a way that it becomes as normal and life giving as breathing. Our ability to serve as instruments of God's reconciliation requires that we pray that God's thoughts inform our own thought process every day.

Surrender to God

Spiritual disciplines provide a means by which we learn to surrender to God's will for our lives. James Earl Massey, in his book, *Spiritual Disciplines: Growth Through the Practice of Prayer, Fasting, Dialogue, and Worship*, writes, "Christian discipline is a way of being obedient; it is faith being exercised, affirming what the believer sees and holds to be the work of God in the soul. Discipline is indeed a human work, but it is a responsive work to the demands of God's grace."[2] A posture of surrender to God's grace, or obedience to God's will, engenders within us a keen sense of how we can pursue reconciliation as ingrained in our way of life.

Samuel Hines discovered early in his ministry what it meant to surrender to God. During a difficult season, he decided to leave the ministry. He explained: "No matter how you describe it, I came to an impasse in my ministry that could have been the end of it all. I left the pastorate and I left Jamaica. I went to England in pursuit of a new vocation and a new style of life. I contemplated studying to become a physician." One afternoon a highly esteemed church leader unexpectedly knocked at Hines' door. He had been the preacher at Hines' ordination service and served as a mentor to the young Hines. The church leader asked, "What has happened to the vows that you made at your ordination?" Hines replied, "I just don't feel anymore that that's the way I ought to go. I've come on some hard times in my own life and some hard times in ministry. It just takes a lot more than I have to be a pastor. I can't attain the high standards I set for myself or achieve at the level of accomplishment expected of me. I just can't do it." After listening to the young man's cry, the seasoned leader said, "Well, maybe you're right. I don't know. I'm here, though, because the Lord gave me a message for you. The Lord said to tell you that 'the calling of God is without repentance'" (see Romans 11:29, KJV).

Samuel Hines reflected on the leader's words, " 'The calling of God is without repentance.' . . . I read a little blurb in a commentary, to the effect that God never changes his mind. We might change ours, but the Lord never changes his." In the Hines' apartment in England there was a small prayer room. Sam said to his wife, Dalineta, "I'm going into that room, and I'm going to stay there until the Lord changes me. I don't care if it takes all day, if it takes all week, if it takes all year—that's what I'm going to do!" Hines recounted the result of his time of prayer in his book *Experience the Power:*

> I was in there for quite a few days, and the Lord heard my prayer. God changed me and let me know he was not changing his mind. That prayer vigil changed my perspective on life. It gave me a new vision and a new hope. . . . I think every Christian must have those kinds of wrestling experiences, when the Lord deals with you directly and personally. God forgives you for your failures. God cleans you up and restores you. He renews your energy and strength. God says, "I still have use for you." . . . God had not changed his mind. I was trying to change mine. I needed to get serious with the Lord and continue to pursue his plan for my life. That is largely why I am still in ministry today.[3]

Samuel Hines' surrender to God's call provided the bedrock foundation for his ministry of reconciliation. Once he let the choice leave his hands, he was open to be led by God—to think God's thoughts. The spiritual discipline of reconciliation invites us to surrender to God for our own healing and restoration, surrender our thoughts so that they can be replaced by God's thoughts, and surrender our will so that we can be used as ambassadors of God's reconciliation. We must attend to first things first.

QUESTIONS FOR DISCUSSION

1. How have you previously defined reconciliation? Compare your definition with the definition offered by Hines.

2. Identify all of the "ghettos" you live in. What are some strategies you can implement to reduce any areas of isolation in your life?

3. What does it mean to think God's thoughts? To think reconciliation?

4. Recall a story or incident that illustrates surrendering to God. What does it mean to surrender to God in the area of reconciliation?

5. Do you agree that reconciliation should be considered a spiritual discipline? Why or why not?

NOTES

1. Howard Thurman, *Disciplines of the Spirit* (Richmond, Ind.: Friends United Press, 1963, 1987), 110.
2. James Earl Massey, *Spiritual Disciplines: Growth Through the Practice of Prayer, Fasting, Dialogue, and Worship* (Grand Rapids: Francis Asbury Press, 1985), 21–22.
3. Samuel G. Hines, *Experience the Power* (Anderson, Ind.: Warner, 1993, 1995), 74–77.

I

The Need for Reconciliation

A Look at a Broad Range of Issues
Facing the First-Century Church at Corinth

SAMUEL GEORGE HINES

NATURAL DISTINCTIONS LIKE RACE, GENDER, AND AGE GROUPINGS, AS well as geographical divisions based on history and politics, splinter our society. The national and cultural settings in which we live are built around traditions, values, and social heritage. Add to this the socioeconomic divide of class, and we begin to understand the instability of our human society. All of these inform our reality. These differences become even more problematic when introduced into the life of the church. These divisions subdivide into smaller units, such as the conflicts found within groups, between leaders and followers (such as pastors and congregations), between various leaders in a church, and ultimately within the hearts of particular men and women. Such ongoing strife points to the original alienation between God and humankind. We do not have to leave our churches to discover that the need for reconciliation is always present. The most crucial work assigned to God's church is reconciliation. Within the body of Christ the church works out the meaning of its existence and finds its most significant and essential focus. The church's call to reconciliation begins within the local congregation.

Reconciliation in the Church

Paul's letters to the Corinthians provide the greatest text for addressing the need for reconciliation in the church. Although properly established and growing, the Corinthian church waded through deep and muddy waters early in its existence. The need for reconciliation was urgent. A quick overview of the Corinthian letters brings to notice a formidable listing of problems in that church. To get a complete picture of the Corinthian situation, one must also review Acts 18 and Paul's entire letter to the Ephesians. If ever a church had problems, the Corinthian church certainly had them.

We label some churches today as "problem" churches. This implies that others are free from difficulties. The truth is that all churches can be called "problem" churches at various times. Budgets and attendance do not tell the whole story. Sometimes the more money and the more people in a congregation, the more those predicaments proliferate. We should not consider ourselves martyrs because we face problematic situations; the first-century congregations also experienced serious dilemmas. Nor should we turn our backs on a church because of its problems. The Corinthian church had many difficulties, some of which we would not even want to mention in our own assemblies. The community's members were converted, baptized with the Holy Spirit, and very gifted, but they had myriad problems, all of which can surface in our congregations today. In this chapter I discuss the following areas in which the Corinthian church needed reconciliation: spiritual maturity, leadership, doctrinal beliefs, gifts and worship, discipline and forgiveness, ethics and behavior, marital status, and race and ethnicity.

Spiritual Maturity

Paul expressed deep concern about the very slow spiritual growth of the people in the Corinthian church (1 Corinthians 2:12–3:3). He compared their lack of understanding of spiritual things to the stunted growth of a child who continues to require soft food rather than food that needs to be chewed. The apostle said that the people's lack of spiritual growth was directly related to their concentration on worldly attitudes, such as envy and jealousy, which led them into contentions and divisiveness. The same remains true for us today. We need godly reconcilers to help us maximize our spiritual growth as we realign our perceptions and reorder our priorities.

A lack of spiritual maturity caused the Corinthian church to have serious moral problems (1 Corinthians 5:1–2,9–13; 6:9–11). Uncontrolled sexual expression developed in the church as many of the ungodly aspects of Greek society continued to invade their lifestyle.

Their behaviors were more in tune with society than with Christ. Now, love was being preached in that church. Unfortunately, the preaching of love can manifest itself in ways we do not intend. This church at Corinth had some strange manifestations of love. They had a glaring need to reconcile their testimony to their lifestyle. The moral situation had sunk so low that a son had trespassed on the sexual territory reserved for his father. He involved himself in an incestuous relationship with his stepmother. Paul dealt with this situation directly by advising strong disciplinary measures. Later he directed the leaders to forgive the brother so that he could be reconciled with the fellowship (2 Corinthians 2:1–11). Reconcilers need divine wisdom.

Paul also identified a large group in that church as being guided by worldly thinking (1 Corinthians 2:1–3:3; 10:20–21). As a result of their spiritual immaturity, they gloried in the flesh and belittled others. Competitiveness caused serious concerns. Paul knew that the church was built on a firm foundation. As he looked on, some constructed unworthy things on that base. He felt ashamed and embarrassed because of what they built. As a leader, when you put all your energies, gifts, and abilities into an effort, you become frustrated and grieved to see someone else come in and erect inferior structures. That happened in Corinth. Because of Paul's inner pain and the resulting confusion in the Corinthian church, reconciliation was necessary.

Some of the Corinthian believers declared that they were not intellectual. Rather, they had knowledge through revelation. Their catch phrase was, "the Lord said . . . , and unfortunately, he did not say this to you but to me." They thought that this gave them a very special platform in the church. When they spoke everyone was compelled to listen, since they had "a word from the Lord." These individuals needed to better understand God's love and way of operation (1 Corinthians 14:26–28). They needed to learn how to practice the reconciliation that they testified to have with God and how to speak the truth in love. Many have been damaged spiritually by individuals who "prophesy" out of their own ego needs, agendas, desire to be viewed as spiritual, and the like. Without the maturity that comes from practicing spiritual disciplines, congregations will find themselves struggling with issues of immorality, worldly thinking, and abusive claims to power through "special" knowledge. We must commit ourselves to holiness and humility so that the ministry of reconciliation will thrive.

Leadership

In addition to spiritual maturity, the Corinthian church had some serious leadership problems. It is amazing how early in its history the church developed difficulties in leadership! Cliques emerged in this church in Corinth (1 Corinthians 3:4–7,21–23). Cliques are not built around doctrines; they develop around personalities. All that is needed for the formation of factions in a congregation is the presence of a few strong personalities to whom people are attracted. We build loyalties around such charismatic people. In the Corinthian church some said, "I am of Cephas (Peter)." That must have been a large group. Some said, "I am of Paul—the original founder." Some said, "I am of Apollos, because he is intellectual and progressive—a little more liberal in his thinking than those others." Some even had the presumption to say, "I am of Christ." This is the worst clique in any church. In this case, people do not perceive themselves as a faction, but see everyone else as being in a clique. Like the Corinthians, they emphasize that they do not follow Peter, Paul, or Apollos, but they follow Christ! They suggest that they have an exclusive relationship with Christ. This belief gives birth to one of the most destructive forces in the body of Christ. The need for reconciliation at this level was paramount in the Corinthian church, as also in our churches today.

In addition to cliques, some in the Corinthian church were determined to undermine Paul himself because he asserted his apostolic leadership (1 Corinthians 4:8–16). God specifically sent Paul to the apostolic ministry among the Gentiles. Yet he ran into conflict with others who declared that God had also sent them to the same places that Paul believed God had sent him (2 Corinthians 11:4–6,16–33; 12:1–15). The primary objective of these new leaders was to cancel the leadership of the apostle Paul. Some pastors have difficulty understanding that individuals may attempt to undermine their authority. Some people do not want the pastor to have the authority that belongs with leadership. They will do everything they can to lessen that authority: gossip, bring false charges against the leader, belittle the leader's ministry, twist whatever he or she says, and contort his or her actions to give messages that the pastor or leader never intended. Paul experienced great pain in this area, because he loved the people in the Corinthian church (2 Corinthians 7:2–4). Leaders who love a group of people agonize when they see them persuaded to follow others who do not have the same depth of love for them. The need for reconciliation becomes very poignant in times like these.

While a pastor must be free to exercise the gifts that God has given him or her, the people are also free (2 Corinthians 1:24; 4:5). They should not regard pastors as undisputed rulers over God's heritage. How can we walk that thin line, that narrow ridge, and bring reconciliation in our churches between pastor and people? All across this country friction and feuding exist between pastors and their congregations. As a result, many congregations have split into two or more factions. How can spiritual leaders reconcile their own selfhood and their God-given authority with the people's freedom? How can leaders exercise their gifts, their anointing, and the authority that flows out of that anointing without trampling on the people of God they serve? How does one reconcile the freedom of the gospel and the discipline that must be exercised? Intense search of the Scriptures, much prayer, face-to-face dialogue, mutual forgiveness, repentance, and a true desire for peace—all of these are necessary for reconciliation to be effected. Godly reconcilers must handle these situations honestly and fairly.

Another problem Paul faced in the Corinthian church regarding leadership surrounded the freeness of the gospel versus the expenses of proclaiming the gospel (1 Corinthians 9:1–14). How does one preach a free gospel and still require a salary? Some people have tremendous conflict in their spirits in this area. Paul had preached that the gospel was free. He had even engaged in the trade of tentmaking to defray some of his expenses. Yet some did not want to give him any remuneration for his labor in the gospel. What should leaders do when people act downright mean to them? Sometimes pastors are doing their best, their spouses also work, their families need help, and the church says (in attitude if not in words), "Keep the pastor poor, and let God keep her or him humble." What does one do with a stingy congregation that will spend money for everything but a pastor's salary? Important factors to consider here are: What are the people's strengths and needs? What are the pastor's needs and the people's expectations of her or him? Despite these concerns, leaders cannot attempt to get money from the people by doubtful maneuvers. That will lead to serious trouble, as we have seen even on our television sets. A posture of reconciliation on both sides would prevent both the pastor and the congregation from disarray, disgrace, or dissolution.

Another charge brought against Paul implied that he was a fickle leader because he changed his mind about certain things he had initiated (1 Corinthians 2:1–8). Some accused him of instability. When such accusations happen often, pastors may refuse to initiate or accommodate change under any circumstances, even when they have to personally acknowledge that they are in error. Every leader should understand that a person can be flexible without being fickle. The ability to change is not a weakness but requires a great deal of strength. Someone has said that it takes supernatural strength to make altogether new beginnings. The leader and the people must be reconciled in their approach to administration. The ambassador of reconciliation will need to be mindful that leadership issues can divide congregations. Therefore, the formation of cliques, attempts at sabotaging pastoral authority, dictatorial pastors, pastoral compensation, and disagreements around administration must be addressed immediately and forthrightly.

Doctrinal Beliefs

Not only did spiritual immaturity and leadership issues divide the church, but some of the Corinthians rallied around one or another of the church's doctrines and practices. Some took a strong stand around baptism. Paul declared how he thanked God that, with a few exceptions, he had not baptized any of them (1 Corinthians 1:14–17). He did not want people tying themselves to him because of some sentimental or ceremonial understanding. Paul had to deal with other problematic areas including beliefs concerning circumcision (1 Corinthians 7:18–20), faith (1 Corinthians 16:13), the resurrection (1 Corinthians 15:12–58), and financial stewardship (1 Corinthians 16:1–2; 2 Corinthians 9:6–8). An urgent need for reconciliation emerges when the letter of the law overshadows the spirit of the law. Some in the Corinthian church found themselves caught up in intellectual disputations over doctrines. These articulate, academic people felt superior in their wisdom, which Paul assessed to be worldly wisdom. While obviously sharp intellectually, their arrogance triggered problems. Like many of us, what they argued about so vehemently may not have been mirrored in their lifestyles. Reconciliation is always an up-front need in these circumstances.

Gifts and Worship

While I have thus far noted several problem areas facing this fellowship, the Corinthian church was a gift-endowed church (1 Corinthians 12:1–14:40). Yet some of these early believers gloried in their gifts just as many Christians do today, causing a colossal problem. Paul acknowledged that the Corinthian church lacked no spiritual gift. We would all like to be part of a church like that! Yet when we find such a church, the problems can become monumental. Questions arise about who does or does not have gifts, who should have gifts and how or when the gifts should be used. Such queries can cause friction. Gifts such as speaking in tongues, prophesying, faith, healing, and administration can build up or break down a fellowship of believers.

Many people in our churches, then and now, have a strange notion that their gifts entitle them to receive special favors and privileges. People rarely link gifts with responsibilities. Rather, they associate gifts with "rights." For example, if someone has the gift of preaching, that person may feel he or she has a right to preach in any service, even if it means displacing the pastor of the church. Someone who claims to have the gift of teaching may think that those who have been teaching previously should sit down. The self-appointed teacher says, "I have the gift." We seem to believe that a gift gives us credentials and licenses that no one can challenge. Some exhibit the attitude, "Do not touch me, for I am gifted." The Corinthian church had serious "gift" problems and needed to learn how to be reconciled to one another so that every gift could be used to edify *all* the people of God.

The multigifted church at Corinth, not surprisingly, had problems in worship (1 Corinthians 11:18–22,33–34; 14:33–35). How do people reconcile their problems surrounding worship? Difficulties had arisen around the observance of the Lord's Supper. They also had a problem between men and women (who in those times sat in separate areas) expressing themselves. Women would shout across to their husbands to find out the meaning of what was preached to establish understanding. Embracing the freedom they had been taught often caused disruption. Today we argue over styles, volume, and varieties of music. Some people declare certain styles deadening while others declare certain kinds disruptive. The call for biblical reconciliation is critical when dealing with the issue of worship.

Discipline and Forgiveness

Another frustration for Paul concerned the lack of discipline exhibited in the Corinthian church (1 Corinthians 4:18–20; 5:3–13). He never compromised with any of it because he so highly valued discipline. Even today the tragedy is not so much the moral lapses in the church or the division and competitiveness among the leaders. No! The real tragedy is that often there are few spiritually called and equipped leaders who have the courage to deal with these problems in the open, according to biblical guidelines. Backsliding (losing one's focus in the center of God's will) necessitates true repentance on the part of the offender and firm, compassionate discipline by a God-appointed leader. These actions should be later followed by reconciling actions of the entire community, leading to restoration of fellowship between all persons involved. Some people believe that the church's weakness is mainly one of doctrine or theology. Careful examination reveals that the weakness centers more in discipline. If we would learn again our responsibility to exercise Christian discipline, both personally and corporately within the church, we could cut out much of the nonsense and divisiveness before it gets to epidemic proportions. Most of us are the victims of our own default. We need to strengthen our own disciplines and handle disciplinary problems with firmness and love, using the biblical prescriptions clearly set out by Jesus and Paul (Matthew 18:15–17; Galatians 6:1; 2 Timothy 2:25–26).

At the same time, Paul is concerned about the overextension of discipline, the exaggeration of discipline, and the prolonging of discipline beyond a reasonably effective period (2 Corinthians 2:1–11). We must not become like demagogues or dictators in the church, exerting frightening authority to cut down anyone who does not please us. Pastors have been known to disfellowship large segments of their congregations when people speak against them. The temptation to be excessive and high-handed in disciplinary matters is as bad as not exerting any discipline at all. Paul laments over the fact that, sometimes in trying to correct and help people, we can destroy them. We must always remember that discipline does not intend to destroy people, but to build them up, to edify, correct, and restore them. Reconciliation always includes repentance, forgiveness, and, when necessary, restoration.

These are situations in which leaders within the body of Christ need to have the ability and willingness to engage in "carefrontation"[1] as detailed by David Augsburger in his book, Caring Enough to Confront. Carefrontation enables us to deal with disciplinary matters from the motivation and perspective of loving concern. Here, the leader is neither trying to harass nor to embarrass the other person, or to win points. The prevailing desire is to help the other person to see God's point of view and accept it for himself or herself.

The apostle Paul found that the Corinthian church also needed reconciliation between the pooled strength of the congregation (the corporate body) and the personal weaknesses of various individuals in that fellowship. Even in the best of times in congregations, when glorious revival occurs and miracles take place, sometimes a brother or sister demonstrates an awful weakness that brings reproach on themselves and everyone else (2 Corinthians 2:1–11). Reconciliation has to take place between the personal concerns and needs of an individual and the common witness of the fellowship.

Ethics and Behavior

Given the lack of clarity about discipline, the Corinthian church also had difficulties in the area of ethics and personal behavior. Paul emphasized that in the area of behavior the question is not merely what is lawful or unlawful (1 Corinthians 6:12–13; 10:23). He declared that many things that we can do lawfully are not advisable. In Washington, D.C., I am regularly exposed to the deliberations of Congress when they select Supreme Court justices. During the selection process, we are often told that judges have a responsibility to find the original intent of the law. Then they have to interpret the findings in contemporary terms and apply them to the current situation, making sure that the application of the law fulfills the original intent. In the church we have to recognize the ethical standards not governed by civil law and apply biblical principles. In the life of the church, when judgment or decisions are made on the bases of irrefutable biblical truths, the people of God all share the responsibility to follow the biblical standard, even if it upsets some persons or goes contrary to the law of the land. The first-century apostles told the ruling authorities, "We must obey God rather than any human authority" (Acts 5:29).

The apostle Paul stated that he had found that, when faced with the issue of the spiritual maturity of others, sacrificial expedience should determine one's choice regarding certain behaviors. The apostle Paul found that expedience determined one's choice regarding some practices. For instance, in that time the eating of meat offered to idols provoked questions, such as "Can I eat meat after it has been defiled by being offered to idols? Can I take it home from the market, pray over it, bless it, and eat it?" (1 Corinthians 8:1–13; 10:19–33). Paul declared that it could be done. The blessing would be honored by God, and what God had blessed no one could curse. Then Paul made the timely observation that because some people had not yet grasped this truth, there should be no flaunting of this practice before them. While it was lawful to eat the meat, wisdom dictated otherwise. The church today has great difficulty in handling such issues. Someone always wants to make laws, a list of "Thou shalts" and "Thou shalt nots." Paul advised against that practice. We do have certain freedoms, but these should not be used to embarrass or confuse other people. We should search the Scriptures diligently for biblical answers to these questions in the "gray" areas of life.

I will expand on this point a bit further. Paul went on to give definitions of weak persons and strong persons (1 Corinthians 10:24–33). We would probably say that the strong person is the one who declares that we should not eat the meat in question. Yet Paul defined that person as being one of the weak ones. The person who can bless the meat and eat it with a clear conscience is one of the strong ones. Such a person, though, should not use his or her strength to destroy others. These decisions may seem to promote a very elastic type of ethics; rather, such situations provide serious challenges to our comprehensive knowledge of Scripture and our spiritual discernment. Reconcilers have to be able to deal with these oft recurring issues by basing decisions on the entire meaning of Scripture rather than on one or two quoted verses.

Further, some bad patterns arose in the church. Christians took each other to the civil courts (1 Corinthians 6:1–8). We do not give any great thought to that kind of action nowadays—it has become commonplace. In the early church, however, it was not allowed. Paul had deep insight regarding this matter. He said in essence that when we, as Christians, take other Christians before the civil judge, we tell the world that not a single wise person resides among us, as believers, who can be a reconciler. When the church begins to give the world the impression that there are no reconcilers left among us, we are in deep trouble. Reconciliation is always possible if there is a mutual desire to seek peace.

Marital Status

Another matter related to ethics and behavior was the need for reconciliation as it related to one's marital status. The sexual ethic within marriage was a problematic area (1 Corinthians 7:2–7). Earlier Paul made reference to sexual problems outside of marriage. Now we find that there were also problems within marriages. Married people did not behave correctly with each other sexually. Even to this day this problem exists at every level of society, in all churches and among people who have been married for varying lengths of time. No one outside of a given marriage, except God, knows what truly happens between a couple. As

Christians, we have to be careful not to deny in the bedroom the testimonies that we make at the altars in our churches. Many of us backslide, not on the streets, but in the privacy of our own personal relationships with our spouses, because our behavior is not saturated with godliness. The sad thing is that when some people in the church want to behave in odd ways sexually, they use the Bible and the name of Christ to justify their bad behavior.

Paul advocated a sexual ethic within marriage that underscored the theory that spouses ought to mutually agree to sexually accommodate each other, with joy, not with malice or manipulative intent, and not denying access to each other's bodies by using arguments based on unilateral decisions. For this reason and because of problems arising from faulty communication and (traditional) role expectations, reconciliation within marriages, including Christian marriages, is still a very present and pressing need.

Paul also talked about the sexual ethic of single people (1 Corinthians 7:8–9,25–38). He discussed the issues of virgins, celibates, and widow(er)s. We need to state clearly today that the single lifestyle is an option. There is nothing wrong with people who choose to be single. We must stop trying to get everyone married. In fact, some of the marriages we have contrived have not been good. We have compelled people into marital union, left them bound to each other while they experience daily strife, and then dared them to dissolve the union through divorce. The apostle Paul also deals with divorce, particularly with divorce between believers and nonbelievers (1 Corinthians 7:10–17). We have a great deal of difficulty with divorce these days. Again, if or when relationships become fractured in these situations, all efforts aimed at reconciliation must focus on responsibilities based on love rather than rights based on law.

Race and Ethnicity

With all of the other issues facing the church in Corinth, we should not be surprised by the existence of issues based on race and ethnicity. Some of the people in the Corinthian church sought to determine who were God's favorites—the Jews or the Gentiles (1 Corinthians 1:22–24; 11:18–19; 12:12–13; 2 Corinthians 5:16). Does this sound like the first century or the present? Reconciliation was as urgently needed then as now. Reconciliation neither denies nor defies our ethnic or racial distinctions. Reconciliation is God's plan for dealing with alienation, conflicts, crises, fragmentation, and polarization in relationships. The primary focus of the process of reconciliation is not centered in cultural or religious issues, land ownership, money, or political power. The focus is, or ought to be, based on our oneness in Christ and directed toward the building or restoration of relationships that facilitate the sharing of complementary resources, for the common good. The launching of projects aimed at effecting reconciliation is one way of "doing" theology, so that we can address the issues that have an impact on contending individuals, communities, or nations. The basis of our fellowship with people is not calculated on the ground of the identities of the flesh (2 Corinthians 5:16). Race, culture, social standing, gender, religious traditions, or economic levels do not have any place as determinants of Christian fellowship. No one should be rated "after the flesh" in the Christian community. We do not even relate to Jesus Christ "after the flesh," that is, in regard to his country of origin, religious background, or the like. He gave his life to make us one.

Beginning at this common level, in Jesus, God established a solution by placing the cross in the center of history—"One died for all" (2 Corinthians 5:14). No person or group receives a special rating. All are equally sinful participants needing the same sacrificial solution. The crucified, resurrected Christ is the magnet that draws all together.

> For he is our peace; in his flesh he has made both groups into one and has broken down the dividing wall, that is, the hostility between us. He has abolished the law with its commandments and ordinances, that he might create in himself one new humanity in place of the two, thus making peace, and might reconcile both groups to God in one body through the cross, thus putting to death that hostility through it. (Ephesians 2:14–16)

Godly reconciliation, then, brings about a radical change in us so that all persons can rightly relate to God the Father, through Jesus Christ the Son, by the power of the Holy Spirit. Having perfected this plan in Christ Jesus, God gave to the reconciled community the message and ministry of reconciliation. Our redemptive and transforming experience gives birth to a ministry to others where we see every person as a candidate for reconciliation. The ministry of reconciliation directs us toward the powerful and powerless, the rich and the poor, the educated and the uneducated. The church as a family, with unity in diversity, bears the responsibility to make reconciliation a manifested reality. God's plan has no room for any church fellowship to be intentionally and exclusively limited to race or other ethnic interests, however historically justified and culturally expedient those divisions may seem to be.

Conclusion

I have discussed at some length the need for reconciliation in the Corinthian church around matters of spiritual maturity, leadership, doctrinal beliefs, gifts and worship, discipline and forgiveness, ethics and behavior, marital status, and race and ethnicity. A need for the ministry of reconciliation within the family of believers exists if a church evidences any of these problems or a combination of several of them. Our congregations need godly leaders, whom Paul refers to as ambassadors of reconciliation. Such leaders do not dodge the issues. Reconciling leaders learn to bend without sacrificing truth or righteousness. They know how to negotiate with all the contending parties. Ambassadors of reconciliation help people to face the causes of estrangement and see the need for (and results of) reconciliation through teaching, counseling, and modeling.

Godly reconcilers bring healing and wholeness instead of brokenness and estrangement. Let me reemphasize that the beauty of Christian churches and groups is not conformity but unity in diversity. We can demonstrate that, as human beings, our similarities greatly outnumber our dissimilarities and we can have unity and plurality at the same time within the same group. We can work together in the essentials, exercise compassionate understanding in the nonessentials, and demonstrate unity in all things. People in the world face alienation every day, they do not need to experience the same brokenness in the church. The church must become a reconciled community of reconcilers who can agree to disagree, when and if necessary, and demonstrate oneness in all things.

QUESTIONS FOR DISCUSSION

1. List as many ways as you can think of that we need reconciliation in our world, in the church, and in our families. In what ways do the needs of reconciliation differ when found in the world—the church—the family? How are they similar?

2. Define spiritual maturity. How does one become spiritually mature? What is the relationship between spiritual maturity, leadership, and the ministry of reconciliation?

3. Given that doctrinal beliefs, spiritual gifts, and worship often cause division (when they are meant to unite), articulate some strategies for reconciliation.

4. How important are ethics and behavior for the Christian? How do ethics and behavior have an impact on the ministry of reconciliation?

5. Of all the issues facing the Corinthian church, which one is most prevalent in your church? Why?

NOTE

1. David Augsburger, *Caring Enough to Confront* (Scottdale, Pa.: Herald Press, 1973, 1981).

2

God's One-Item Agenda

The Central Focus of
God's Word and Works

SAMUEL GEORGE HINES

HISTORY IS ON COURSE AND HEADING GOD'S WAY. EVEN WHILE THE NEED for reconciliation in the church and society is great, the divine one-item agenda unfolds in God's salvation history. God's agenda must become our agenda. God's agenda is serious business dominated by a divine unifying purpose. Both in creation and in redemption, the reconciling plan prevails in the divine drama. Whether the stage is in heaven or on the earth, God's goal is oneness. History records our divisions and subdivisions. Fragmentation exists as a cardinal feature of human life. Given time, all things break up and fall apart into smaller particles. Our human efforts alone do not hold us together for any appreciable length of time. But God's agenda focuses on reconciliation, which leads to lasting unity and oneness.

God's agenda calls attention to the central, unique, and sovereign operation in creation, in history, and in all eternity. It acknowledges not only that God is deliberately, intentionally, and purposefully at work in this global arena, but also that the church is God's chosen partner in the administration of what the apostle Paul incisively called, "the mystery." He wrote: "In him we have redemption through his blood, the forgiveness of our trespasses, according to the riches of his grace that he lavished on us. With all wisdom and insight he has made known to us the mystery of his will, according to his good pleasure that he set forth in Christ, as a plan for the fullness of time, to gather up all things in him, things in heaven and things on earth" (Ephesians 1:7–10). Messianic prophecies from the Old Testament, coupled with a close study of the New Testament, will clearly reveal many riveting facts about Jesus, the Son of God and Son of man. One of those shining truths is that in the earthly life of Jesus, all the miracles of healing, feeding, deliverance from demons and raising of dead persons to life are evidences of God's power and purpose to bring unity, wholeness and reconciliation between God and human beings, within individual bodies and spirits and between one person and another.

As a student of the Bible for the vast majority of my years, I confess openly that I do not know how to consider such matters as "divine agenda," "God's agenda," "sovereign purpose," and "the church's mandate," without climbing to the uppermost summits and walking onto the outermost limits of revealed truth as found in the grandest and most majestic of all Paul's letters—the epistle to the Ephesians. Here, in this apostolic circular, Paul clarifies and celebrates God's exalted vision from this peak of revelation, encompassing the panoramic view of God's wondrous works in all their kaleidoscopic glory. The apostle is escorted by the Spirit up to the highest altitudes of revelation, and the curtain is drawn back to unveil the ultimate vision of what is referred to five times (and only in this letter) as "heavenly places." Walk reverently here, my friend. You are not only on the highest point of revelation, you are gazing into the brightest "Son" of illumination! Slow down! Blink if you must!

I was driving along the New England Thruway early one morning when the blazing brilliance of the early morning sun blinded me to the traffic around me. My beloved wife said, "Slow down, honey; you're driving into the sun." And that is what we are going to do in this chapter—drive into the Son. Let us behold the brilliant, scintillating jewels of this text in Ephesians as it gives us a picture of the divine agenda.

Sufficiency

The first gem in this arrangement of jewels is sufficiency. God's agenda includes the most superlative and superabundant blessings. Paul lists many blessings, including redemption, forgiveness, and the plenitude of God's providential provision for us. The divine agenda supplies all our needs according to God's riches in glory through Christ Jesus. Redemption through Christ's blood is full salvation! That is liberation at its best! As I like to remind people when I preach:

Redemption is deliverance from
all that is binding, blighting, blinding, and burdensome to our natures,
all that is chaffing, cheapening, and crippling in our lives,
all that is deadening, demeaning, and depressing to our spirits,
all that is encumbering, enslaving, and ensnaring to our physical beings,
and all that is lessening, limiting, and loading of our personhood.
God's grace redeems, refurbishes, renews, replaces, and replenishes.
That is God's agenda.
It is Satan who depletes, deprives, diminishes, and dismantles.
Satan is the culprit who drains you out and dries you up.

This is radical! Sin—disobedience to God—creates divisions, separations, alienations, polarizations, and fragmentations. Sin splits us up into conflicting camps and plants hostility in our hearts. Sin breeds fear, discrimination, bitterness, and illogical, irrational prejudices. All of these spin-offs of sin hinder reconciliation and solidarity. Sin tears up, disrupts, disconnects, and puts us at odds with one another.

Paul also declared that there was forgiveness on God's agenda. What a blessing! We are assured that God will forgive our sins and bear them so far away that they never come back to haunt us or hurt us again. There is so little forgiveness in the world today. Sometimes even in the church forgiveness is a scarce commodity. There is also a great deal of vindictiveness, punitive behavior, and hostility among human beings. But God offers us redemption and forgiveness. In what measure do we receive this? In accordance with the measure or riches of *God's* grace. Now that is sufficiency! The apostle said that God's grace was "lavished on us" (1:8). God does not want to bless us by giving just a little drop here or there. God wants to lavish blessings upon us. The King James Version of the Bible uses the word "abounded" when referring to the overflow that is ours in the abundant life. Sufficiency (more than enough) is a feature of God's provision, and adequacy is an essential part of God's sufficiency. If you need it, God has it. Ask and wait for God's outpouring. (See Matthew 7:7, John 15:7, and James 4:2.)

Sovereignty

Another gem that we observe in this bright shining diadem is *sovereignty*. Paul wrote that God "has made known to us the mystery of his will, according to his good pleasure that he set forth in Christ" (1:9). When we talk about the dispensation of the fullness of times or seasons, and God's providence and preeminence in gathering all things together, we imply a perspective on history that goes far beyond calendars, dates, and generations. We deny the claims of humanism and secularism. We acknowledge that God is sovereign and soars above our human limitations. When we confess God's sovereignty, we proclaim that history is more than the story of what has happened—the lining up of events; the successions of movements; reformations and revolutions; wars won and wars lost; and the rise and fall of civilizations, empires, and nations. We recognize that history is more than the emergence and disappearance of heroes and heroines, demigods and dictators; more than the birth and death of institutions; more than the line up of trends and fashions, ideologies, and philosophies; more than the speeches of eloquent men and women; more than the rise and fall of charismatic leaders. We acknowledge that history is more than moral mood swings and emotional merry-go-rounds, more than the records of our experiences, mistakes, and successes. God's sovereignty goes beyond all these considerations.

Our recognition of the divine agenda affirms that we live in God's world. God is the creator and owner of everything, and he is in control of history. God bends the arc of the universe toward the divine purpose every day. God is not just filling out calendars and keeping diaries; he administers the seasons of history, controls the currents of time, arranges the spans as well as what seems to be the spontaneity of our days, and presides over the completeness, rather than the fragmentation of human affairs. God is still on the throne!

Some unbelievable things happened within the last half of the twentieth century. The maps of the world were redrawn. Political winds blew in some strange directions. Alignments shifted. In Europe and in the Middle East new geopolitical developments are emerging. New persons are proclaiming and putting into practice new schema for church growth and management. Not only did the communist system fall apart, but our capitalistic economy also shows signs of dis-ease. Leaders talk about a "new world order." Where is God in all of this? Is God somewhere on the sidelines watching things unveil? Is God a spectator in this vast expanse of the universe? Is God in exile, a refugee from the world? Was God voted out of office? Did God retire as a "God emeritus," favored with title but lacking any authority? However loudly we may answer *NO!* to these questions, that will not be enough. If God's agenda is to become our mandate, then we must begin all over again to submit to God our minds, our perceptions, our plans, our relationships, our ventures, and our visions. We must bring them all under God's sovereignty. We must begin again by saying *YES!* to the sovereignty and supremacy of God.

We have become so accustomed to challenging everything in our society that we even challenge God Almighty, the sovereign, supreme one who is credited with the final consummation of all things. I once read an article on evil that reminded readers of the theologian's plight in declaring some conflicting affirmations: (1) God is all-powerful, (2) God is all-good, and (3) terrible things happen (in our bodies, in nature, and in society). These three statements do not seem to match. The existence of evil, its prevalence and indiscriminate assault on good people, bad people, innocent people, even babies, presents us with legitimate questions that deserve answers we may not receive or understand on this side of eternity. The recent wars and continuing violence in the Middle East, Central Europe, African nations, and other places raise many questions that we must all face. The moral overtones of our responses in these situations have not been appropriately addressed by any of us. The questions here are not just what we should do now, and should or should not have done in the past. The question we must ask ourselves is, "What is God doing?" In seeking for answers, we should not try to squeeze God into a mold of our own making and reduce the Almighty to our explainable level of understanding. We have to keep our minds and spirits open to receive the enlightenment of the Holy Spirit, who, "will lead us into all truth" (John 16:13).

Many of us struggle with very personal and intimate issues. Some of us are puzzled about what is happening in our nation and economy, in our jobs and professions, in our health and the aging process, in the lives of our young people and families, and in our churches. In all of this the Christian affirms that God is neither weak nor indifferent. God is not in exile, although many have tried to shove the Almighty off the stage. People and nations that dismiss God from the arena of their lives find themselves in a godless place of their own choosing. That does not, however, address the problem of the good people who die from cancer, or from the ravages of nature in places like Bangladesh, or in plane crashes, or who develop AIDS, and other such calamities. This includes innocent people born with disabilities or genetic problems. Remember that Job asked the same type of questions. (Read God's answer in Job 38–41.)

Paul reminds us that God's agenda offers wisdom, discernment, understanding, intelligence, and prudence, and it reveals secrets to us

concerning *who* God is and *how* God operates. Not all our squeamish-
ness nor all our impatience, and not all the forces of evil and their repul-
sive manifestations in life can manipulate God's agenda. God is the
master household manager whose wisdom and authority order and
arrange the household and plan everything.

In the fullness of time, Jesus came to bring us back to oneness with
God. In due season, when everything is in place, the sovereign God will
make a strategic move to bring all things together in Christ Jesus, finally
vindicating truth and righteousness and ultimately dethroning and
destroying evil. For us here and now, the spiritual warfare continues as
the battle is waged between the forces of good and evil. There are many
casualties, but for the true believer, there is no doubt as to who now has
and always will have the upper hand and the last word. God has taken
the initiative and works in the world creatively restoring and reordering
this universe. God runs into opposition from Satan but never panics,
because the divine plan is intact and on track.

This revealed plan is a person—Jesus Christ! I remember speaking to
a friend of mine in Washington, D.C., who had just returned from Mongolia. He said to me on the telephone, "Sam, you have got to hear this.
I was in Mongolia with some people, and I was talking about Jesus. Very
few people in Mongolia have ever heard that Jesus exists. As I talked
about Jesus, people began to cry, hug themselves, and hold on to each
other. One man dragged me aside—a great leader in Mongolia—and
said, 'You know something, I have always known in my heart that there
was somebody like that, but I never knew his name. Tell me more about
Jesus.' " You and I have the responsibility to receive this revealed plan in
faith and in submission and proclaim it to the entire world. God's
agenda, then, includes sufficiency with regard to our needs and absolute
sovereignty in the ultimate pursuit of the purpose as it appears in the
"mystery." Let us not get caught up with trying to get around God,
whether it is in our personal lives or in our homes, in our local churches
or in our communities, in our nation or in our world. We must bow to
God's sovereignty.

Solidarity

The last jewel is *solidarity*. We must understand this word very clearly.
What really is God's plan?—"To bring all things in heaven and on earth
together under one head, even Christ" (1:10, NIV). To what end then are

the sufficiency and sovereignty of God at work? Surely God's purpose is to reconcile us so that oneness can be established. Paul said in Ephesians that God wants to bring together all things in Christ. The Greek word for "bringing together" is *anakephalaiosasthai.*[1] The English word that best captures the full meaning of this Greek word is *reconciliation,* and it is the key word for God's agenda. Whenever you question me— even if you were to wake me up at two o'clock in the morning—about what God is doing, I should have one answer for you: God is bringing all things together in Christ. That is God's agenda. Paul expressed a similar thought in Colossians: "For in him all the fullness of God was pleased to dwell, and through him God was pleased to reconcile to himself all things, whether on earth or in heaven, by making peace through the blood of his cross" (1:19–20).

Solidarity does not come easily or automatically. Solidarity will only happen as we are reconciled to God through the sacrifice of Jesus on the cross of Calvary. Then we become empowered through the work of the Holy Spirit to be reconciled to each other.

Before time began God had a purpose in mind, a secret but significant purpose. The incarnation of Jesus—this mind of God, this Word of God made flesh—made God's plan public. In Christ, God revealed that seasons of time are controlled by the divine will, so that in the fullness of time, God can fulfill his purpose to head up all things in heaven and on earth in Christ. This may be the most explosive idea that has ever reached the human mind. God had to keep that idea quiet for ages, secretly operating by it but withholding the revelation until the *kairos* moments—the fullness of time—had come.

One of the major impacts of this idea was that both Jew and Gentile now belonged to the same family through Jesus Christ. The walls of division fell down, and all barriers to solidarity were removed when Jesus came. Servants were made into sons and daughters. Many new children were brought into the family, including the Gentiles. All of the dividing lines were eliminated. They are gone, whether we like it or not! If we try to replace them, we fight a losing battle, and none of us wants to be caught trying to build up what God tore down. Divisions, inequities, and injustice based on age, race, culture, gender, social status, or economic position were removed in Christ. We who live in this period must continue Christ's action. God's goal all through the centuries has been to bring together under Christ Jesus all things in heaven and on earth.

History has not been just one upheaval after another nor a sequence of emergencies. Nor has history been just one big roller-coaster ride with ups and downs—the rhythmic swing from boredom most of the time to excitement now and then. Mere spinning around in space is not the story of our lives. Let us proclaim this to people who are about to lose faith in solidarity. Let us tell it to those trapped in purposeless living and hopeless drifting on this rotating planet we call Earth. Let us announce that God has been, and is, working the divine purpose out—that is the Christian interpretation of history, ancient and modern. History came of age when Jesus arrived on earth. Therefore, the era of time beginning with his birth is referred to as the "fulness of time" (Galatians 4:4, KJV). With Jesus' coming into the world, God announced and released the secret of the ages. That secret is God's plan to establish cosmic unity in this universe, to bring about a christocentric unity in which Jesus gathers together in one, things in heaven and things on earth. Repeatedly, the apostle Paul makes the point that *Christ is the head!*

Through Christ, God's one-item agenda heads up a new solidarity— a new reconciled covenant community. God has a new order that is not racial or national, Jewish or Gentile, Eastern or Western. It is a system of rating based on our reconciliation to God and to each other. We are surely going to miss many steps and lose a lot of time in all our strategy, planning, and programming if we do not get this truth of our theology straight. We mess up when we develop our own speculations and prejudices and refuse to see people as God sees them—all equal in value and all one in Christ. God's universal church is either going to demonstrate this solidarity or become a contemporary scandal, bringing blame and shame to the gospel by virtue of blatant contradictions between what we preach and what we practice.

Of course, the issues no longer center only on Jew and Gentile; they revolve around African American and white, Latino and Asian, native and immigrant, right and left, conservative and liberal, militarist and pacifist. The separatist arguments in the church focus on whether we are movemental; reformational; sectarian; denominational; pre-, post-, or a-millennial; Pentecostal; charismatic; or evangelical. They even focus on the use of traditional or contemporary music and on worship styles. These things send us heading in different directions and getting into our little boxes with divisive labels.

We also create and promote a dichotomy between what some among us label as social gospel on one side (and I am identified as one of the chief transgressors in this area, because we try to feed, clothe, and evangelize the poor) and evangelism on the other, as if those two are exclusively separate. And even among those in social camps, arguments occur as to whether we should do compassionate ministry or advocacy, or work for radical change of governmental systems; whether we are going to be priestly/pastoral in the church or should also be prophetic in our preaching. We spend precious time debating about whether we should be trapped in our American individualism or become more sensitive to our international connections. So we frustrate ourselves by multiplying caucuses, committees, conferences, seminars, symposia and workshops, without coming to conclusive resolutions. We therefore do very little, if any, follow-up with definitive actions and consequently find ourselves unable to maximize the reconciling encounters in which we engage.

What is Christ reconciling in heaven and on earth? How far can we go with cultural domination and still be under Christ the one head? Can we perpetuate racial division and still be under Christ? Do we want to be part of what God puts together, or would we rather organize our own operation and head it up ourselves? How do we balance authority and autonomy in the nation or in the church without getting out of line in our local independence or becoming top-heavy in our centralization? How much diversity can we have within this solidarity, this reconciled community, which is God's plan for all and the principle by which the kingdom of God operates? Paul is saying to the church that God's agenda—our mandate—is to be reconciled to God and to each other and to be united in our diversity through Jesus Christ. We must make the agenda known and make it credible by our behavior.

The church must never allow cultural concerns or institutional interests to override God's agenda of reconciliation, oneness, and solidarity. We can continue to plan our evangelistic campaigns, missionary outreach, church growth strategies, and Christian education programs, but until we acknowledge the error of our ways and a spirit of repentance is poured out on the church, nothing of lasting, godly significance is going to happen. One of the hardest things to get many churchgoers to do is to repent. Some of our traditions have drummed into us that because we are committed to holiness, we never need to repent. One of the things that is destroying the witness and effectiveness of the church today is our lack of repentance.

As God's people, we must discard our own agendas and get on God's agenda. We must repent of everything happening in our hearts that defies the solidarity of God and blocks the reconciling process. We must repent of our indifference to estrangement and injustice. We must repent of everything that happens in our homes that conflicts with God's agenda. We must repent of everything in our local congregations that would nullify reconciliation and hinder the solidarity that God intends us to have. We must repent of everything that has developed in our communities and regions that cuts us off from this solidarity. We must repent of all that has developed in our national and local church agencies that undermines this solidarity. We must renounce attitudes, traditions, customs, and structures that embarrass and compromise our testimony of reconciliation and solidarity. Everything that we do and say in our conferences, dialogues, and deliberations must honor God's agenda. All the decisions that we make, as well as the motivations for our actions and the dedication of our influence, possessions, spiritual gifts, talents, and time for God's service are stimulated by our experience of God's amazing grace, and this brings us all together in solidarity under our one head, who is Jesus Christ. (See Colossians 1:12–17.) We must stand firmly on the foundations of unity and holiness, solidarity and sanctification, reconciliation and refining.

Let us embrace the scandal of our confession and take the risk of our open, naked profession of faith. Let us not fritter away the glory of our consecration as God's partners and workers. God is still moving history toward its final consummation, when Jesus Christ—God's solidarity plan—will be recognized, acknowledged, and confessed universally.

> Therefore God also highly exalted him
>   and gave him the name
>   that is above every name,
> so that at the name of Jesus
>   every knee should bend,
>   in heaven and on earth and under the earth,
> and every tongue should confess
>   that Jesus Christ is Lord,
>   to the glory of God the Father.
>   —*Philippians 2:9–11*

QUESTIONS FOR DISCUSSION

1. After reading this chapter, how would you define and describe God's agenda?

2. Define sufficiency, sovereignty, and solidarity. Why are these important attributes in the divine agenda?

3. Do you believe that God is in control of history? If so, how does that relate to your view of current events? If not, why not?

4. What is the role of Jesus Christ in God's agenda?

5. Why does Samuel Hines say that reconciliation is God's one-item agenda?

NOTE

1. According to Francis Foulkes, *Ephesians,* Tyndale New Testament Commentaries (Leicester, England: Inter-Varsity; and Grand Rapids: Eerdmans, 1956; reprint 1983), 52–53, "Three ideas are present in the word here—restoration, unity, and the headship of Christ."

3

An On-site Job of Reconciliation

Jesus Christ Is God's Reconciler
Par Excellence

CURTISS PAUL DEYOUNG

Sᴀᴍᴜᴇʟ ʜɪɴᴇꜱ ᴄᴏᴍᴍɪᴛᴛᴇᴅ ʜɪꜱ ʟɪꜰᴇ ᴛᴏ ᴍɪɴɪꜱᴛʀʏ ᴀꜱ ᴀ ᴛᴇᴇɴᴀɢᴇʀ ɪɴ Savanna-la-mar, Jamaica, after which he moved to the capital city, Kingston, to find work so that he could afford to go to the university. His parents cautioned their son that moving to the city might adversely impact his spiritual life. His mother expressed particular concern that he might fall prey to the various temptations that abounded in the big city. To address his mother's anxiety and to enrich his own walk with God, Sam Hines involved himself in the Saturday night Youth for Christ events in Kingston. Despite his best efforts, one night as he traveled to an evening service of Youth for Christ, a prostitute propositioned him. Hines recounted the incident: "I discovered for the first time in my life what a prostitute was. Here was a young woman all dressed up accordingly and painted up offering me her body. And I want to tell you that was a shocker! Well I knew enough to resist her and tell her that I was a Christian, and that I was going to Youth for Christ."

When Sam Hines left the meeting, the same woman approached him a second time. "She was there, and she was telling me what a good time she could give me. She was telling me how she liked the color of my eyes, and she was really going to town on me." Hines continued, "Right there and then I could hear my mother's voice saying, 'You're going to go to the bad city and get seduced and become worldly and ungodly and forget your promise to God.'. . . So I resisted the prostitute and went home." This incident had an impact on Samuel Hines' call to ministry. He wondered, *"Who's witnessing to such people? Who is taking them the good news?. . .* The more I thought about it, the more concern I began to develop for people, and particularly for those like that prostitute lady who seemed so mixed up in her purpose in life."[1]

Samuel Hines understood that Jesus came to demonstrate God's concern for people like the woman he encountered on the streets of Kingston. Dr. Hines reminded us in chapter 2 that the centerpiece of God's agenda was the coming of Jesus Christ. In a later chapter he calls this event "an on-site job of reconciliation."[2] Here I will describe the importance and impact of Jesus Christ—God's on-site job of reconciliation—on people in his day and show how these first-century events offer a word for us today.

In the midst of Roman oppression, dehumanizing poverty, ethnic strife, class hatred, disenfranchisement of women, and alienation in numerous other categories of relationships, God sent Jesus to do an on-site job of reconciliation. Although the prophets foretold this on-site job of reconciliation, it was the angel Gabriel who first announced God's new action on earth. He shared the good news in separate interviews with a young engaged couple with the names Mary and Joseph. Gabriel told Mary and Joseph that while they had made the right decision to "just say no" to premarital sex, God had decided that this was the right time to do an on-site job of reconciliation. Therefore, the Holy Spirit had been dispatched to insure that Jesus, the reconciler par excellence, would begin to take form inside Mary's womb. Although this action did not coincide with the plans of Mary or Joseph, they embraced God's will. Then at the appointed hour, Mary and Joseph welcomed the arrival of Jesus and wrapped him in swaddling clothes and laid him in a manger.

As a result of God's on-site job of reconciliation, for thirty-three years people from all walks of life, all races and ethnic groups, all social and economic classes, both women and men, and even angels and demons proclaimed the name of Jesus. A man hanging on a cross next to Jesus, convicted of crimes against the Roman Empire, was the last person to call Jesus by name during his earthly ministry. He said, "Jesus, remember me when you come into your kingdom" (Luke 23:42). Below, we will see how through this on-site job of reconciliation in Jesus, God demonstrated that reconciliation means crossing human-made boundaries, creating empowering relationships, and offering compassion-filled forgiveness.

Crossing Boundaries

The birth of Jesus in Bethlehem crossed the boundary separating the human and the divine. When sin entered the world, a boundary was erected that severed the intimate relationship between God and the first human couple, Adam and Eve. The arrival of Jesus signaled the beginning of the end of this separation, which was completely destroyed in his death and resurrection. The "Jesus event"—birth, life, death, resurrection, and abiding presence—also served as a dramatic reminder of the original oneness God intended for the human family. One cannot miss this message in the Christmas narratives. Poor shepherds from the local community in Palestine and wealthy travelers from distant regions of Asia visited Jesus. Joseph, Mary, and Jesus then journeyed to parts of Africa to find refuge. Geographic boundaries were crossed in God's on-site job of reconciliation. Recall also that Jesus was born and lived most of his life in Palestine, the land bridge connecting Africa and Asia, and located in very close proximity to Europe. God's choice of a site for this visitation did not occur by chance.

Jesus' family descended from the Hebrew people. Africans, Asians, and indigenous people of Palestine populated the family trees of many Hebrews. We could surmise that Jesus had a multicultural or multiracial heritage. Some scholars identify Jesus of Nazareth as an Afro-Asiatic Jew.[3] It is also important to remember that Jesus was raised in Galilee, home to people from Assyria, Babylon, Egypt, Macedonia, Persia, Rome, and Syria, as well as indigenous Canaanites. People from every nation that had colonized Palestine lived in Galilee. Jesus grew up in a multicultural, multiethnic, and international neighborhood. Can you think of a better place for the reconciler par excellence to grow up? Given this fact, it should not surprise us that Jesus would be multilingual. The language that enabled him to communicate to the wide range of people living in Galilee would have been Greek, the language of his people was Aramaic, and the language of the temple was Hebrew. That would make Jesus at least trilingual. (Perhaps Jesus even spoke some of the languages of his neighbors in Galilee.) God's on-site job of reconciliation crossed the boundaries of race, culture, and language.

God's on-site job of reconciliation also crossed the boundary that separated the powerful and the powerless. The apostle Paul articulated this
when he wrote:

> Let the same mind be in you that was in Christ Jesus,
>   who, though he was in the form of God,
>   did not regard equality with God
>   as something to be exploited,
>   but emptied himself,
>   taking the form of a slave,
>   being born in human likeness.
>   And being found in human form,
>   he humbled himself
>   and became obedient to the point of death—
>   even death on a cross.
> —*Philippians 2:5–8*

The all-powerful God entered history as a first-century Palestinian
Jew oppressed by the power of the Roman Empire. His death occurred
through a form of capital punishment designed to bring shame and
humiliation to its victim. Both the powerful and the powerless can identify with Jesus.

In this on-site job of reconciliation, God crossed the boundaries
established by society to keep women powerless. The narratives
describing the birth of Jesus highlight the prominent roles played by
Mary and Elizabeth in the salvation story. Their strength, resourceful-
ness, and partnership are not only noticed, but celebrated by male
gospel writers who easily could have been blinded by the sexism of society. Jesus included women followers in prominent positions in his ministry. Women secured the funds necessary for operational expenses, and
Mary and Martha provided their home as Jesus' primary ministry base.
And women served as the principal witnesses to the most significant
event in the history of humanity—Jesus' resurrection.

In his life and ministry, Jesus modeled God's one-item agenda of reconciliation. His preaching and teaching contained imagery that encouraged
people in his society to embrace God's inclusive love. Jesus reached across
human-made boundaries and invited people to come from east and west
and north and south to join him for a meal at God's table. Even at Jesus'
death, God's on-site job of reconciliation effected a crossing of boundaries
when an African carried the cross and a European proclaimed his faith.[4]

Crossing Boundaries: A Samaritan Case Study

No more powerful example of Jesus crossing boundaries can be found than in the story told in John 4:4–42. That day Jesus traveled one of the seldom-used roads in Samaria. A weary woman whose life as we shall see was a living hell, also walked on one of those lonely lanes in Samaria. These two people who met at Jacob's well lived in a society that had done everything possible to isolate them from each other. Biblical scholar James Earl Massey once said to me that the woman from Samaria was a "boundary person." First-century Palestinian society erected boundaries that were not to be crossed. Societal norms and religious dictates instructed people to know their place and stay in it. The woman Jesus met at the well that day was a "boundary person."

The first boundary society erected to keep Jesus and the Samaritan woman apart was a barrier of cultural or racial classism. The dividing line was very clear: Jesus was a Jew and the woman was a Samaritan. According to first-century religious law, Jewish rabbis were not to cross this boundary Thus, for Jesus, the Samaritan woman was out-of-bounds. Tensions based on issues of race and culture separated them. As I noted in my book *Coming Together: The Bible's Message in an Age of Diversity:*

> When the Israelites were taken into captivity, left behind in the region of Samaria were poor and working-class Hebrews who intermingled with their captors. When the captives returned to Palestine, they sought an advantage through the claim that the Hebrews living in Samaria had inter-married with the colonizers. Not unlike oppressed people in other eras, the people of Samaria had their own story. They claimed that they were the descendants of the patriarch Joseph and his African wife, whose off-spring had become the half-tribes of Ephraim and Manasseh. A rivalry between the returning captives (Jews) and the working-class Hebrews (Samaritans) developed.[5]

The Samaritans knew economic deprivation, and they were on the lowest rung of the social ladder. They were the untouchables of Palestine. An extremely intense hatred existed between the Jews and the Samaritans that reached a fever pitch during the early years of the first century. As a demonstration of their discontent, Samaritan revolutionaries placed human bones in the sanctuary of the Jewish temple in Jerusalem, attempting to defile the worship at the Passover Feast.[6] Urban unrest, ethnic tensions, racial rebellions, civil strife, and unrestrained rioting are not modern inventions. Ignored by their Jewish neighbors and by colonial Rome, Samaritans were an unheard people in the first century.

Two other barriers blocked interaction between Jesus and this woman from Samaria. Gender was a boundary placed by society to keep Rabbi Jesus separated from this woman. Women were held in very low esteem during the first century. Some rabbis of the time made statements such as:

- "One should not talk with a woman on the street, not even his own wife, and certainly not with somebody else's wife because of the gossip of men."[7]

- "It is forbidden to give a woman any greeting."[8]

- "Better to burn the Torah, than teach it to women."[9]

Some first-century Jewish men would even recite the prayer, "Blessed art thou, O Lord…who hast not made me a woman."[10] Another boundary was lifestyle. Jewish religious law allowed for remarriage after a divorce, but at the most, women could marry three times.[11] This woman from Samaria, however, had married five times and had finally chosen to live with a man who was not her husband. Religious society declared her out-of-bounds because of her lifestyle choices.

To make it worse, the woman from Samaria not only experienced outcast status in Jewish society, but her own people despised her as well. While most women in her community drew water in the cool of the morning or evening, she would get her water at noon, the hottest part of the day. It seemed that the whole world labeled her undesirable. Because she did not perceive herself as good enough for Jesus, she asked Jesus why he would talk to her. Society declared her a boundary person, and she internalized this assessment. She hurt emotionally and spiritually.

We live in a society today that has developed a number of boundaries to keep us isolated from each other. Race, culture, gender, class, and lifestyle separate us. Our choices regarding where we live, worship, and socialize offer evidence of this fact. These barriers damage people on both sides of the boundary emotionally, psychologically, socially, physically, and spiritually.

On that day recorded by the Gospel writer John, when the woman from Samaria walked to Jacob's well, she felt weary from her own life's journey. That changed when she met this Jesus who crossed boundaries and removed barriers. Many in Palestine were isolated by life's circumstances. No one related to them until Jesus crossed the boundaries.

When Jesus crossed the line dividing Galilee and Samaria, he chose a path few took. Rather, most Jews traveled around Samaria when going from Galilee to Judea. It required extra time, but that way one could avoid contact with the Samaritans. (I wonder if we build beltways around our cites, in part, to avoid contact with central city neighborhoods?) John 4:4 says that Jesus "had to go through Samaria." Jesus felt compelled to use that route. He went to Samaria because he saw sisters and brothers. If Jesus traveled around Samaria, he would be turning his back on the needs of his family.

Whenever we avoid contact with people from a certain part of our city or town, people from a particular race or economic class, people who make lifestyle choices different from our own, we turn our backs on a part of our family. When we ignore members of the human family, we reject the God in whose image all of humanity is created. If we discover ourselves avoiding places and people, we must, like Jesus, respond to the call of our sisters and brothers in the human family. They need us and we need them. We must not allow any boundary to keep us apart.

Creating Relationships

Jesus crossed the boundaries imposed by society, and so should we. After Jesus crossed boundaries, he created relationships—often at the dinner table. An interesting group of people joined him there, most often people whom no one else would invite over to eat: Samaritans, tax collectors, "sinners," and women. Certain religious leaders were not happy with his dining practices and table manners, saying in essence, "Why does he eat with *those people?* What's wrong with this Jewish rabbi? Doesn't he know the rules?" Jesus knew all the rules, and he broke every one that separated people. Of course Jesus also dined with religious leaders and the powerful. He welcomed everyone at his table, because God was doing an on-site job of reconciliation.

As Jesus invited people to his table, he realized that a truly authentic relationship requires that we understand the experience of the other person. As we know from the episode with the Samaritan woman, Jesus knew how to listen. He learned much about her by simply listening to what she had to say, and he asked the right kind of questions to prompt revealing responses. By listening, Jesus developed some points of reference for understanding the woman. His own human experience must have provided him with ways of connecting with her. Jesus could use his experience as a Jew colonized by Rome to understand her experience as an oppressed Samaritan. Jesus experienced life as one who faced injustice because of his ethnic origin. He understood from a human perspective what it was like to grow up as an outsider in the dominant culture. He had no rights in colonial Rome. Jesus fully understood in his human existence the degradation, the humiliation, the tragedy, the fear, the anger, the outrage, and the despair that the woman from Samaria experienced every day.

When we seek to create relationships with people whose life experience appears different than our own, we must learn to see life through their eyes. We can use our own experience as a resource for gaining this understanding. Have you ever felt isolated? Have you ever felt discouraged? Have you ever felt like no one cared? We can use aspects of our own life in tandem with a disciplined listening ear to gain a sense of what others are experiencing. We must gain points of reference for understanding if we are going to create lasting, meaningful relationships.

Jesus also understood that relationships are based on mutuality. When we create relationships with other people, they must be mutual and not condescending. Jesus demonstrated this mutuality when he asked the woman from Samaria for a drink of water from Jacob's well. Observing her vulnerability (drawing water at noon), Jesus made himself vulnerable. Rabbi Jesus spoke to the woman from Samaria in a public place. As biblical scholar Craig Keener notes, "Asking water of a woman could be interpreted as flirting with her—especially if she had come alone due to a reputation for looseness. Jesus breaks all the rules of Jewish piety here."[12] Jesus risked misunderstanding by the woman (and others) since he did not follow religious dictates. Yet he needed to break free from the customs of the day to demonstrate his interest in her soul. Jesus' actions shocked his disciples but helped prepare the woman to trust him.

Asking for a drink also expressed Jesus' intent for the relationship to be mutual. Jesus came bearing the priceless gift of salvation, but he knew that this woman from Samaria needed to give something to him. Then Jesus gave her a gift. He did not give her a second-hand item; he shared with her something that he had told no one else up to this point in his ministry. He had not told his family, his disciples, his inner circle (Peter, James, and John), the theologian Nicodemus, or anyone else in

Israel. Yet in the midst of creating a relationship with the woman by Jacob's well, he shared with her his very essence. He revealed to her that he was the Messiah (4:25–26). Jesus gave her his best gift!

As we create relationships, they must not only be mutual, they must also be empowering. The woman from Samaria became the first evangelist of the Christian era. She experienced the power of transformation and felt empowered to lead others to her source of liberation. She was a highly credible witness to what the power of God can do. The true test of any ministry is how many of the evangelized become evangelists, how many of the powerless become empowered for leadership. If we read on in John 4, we learn that Jesus and his disciples spent two days in Samaria fellowshipping because of this relationship Jesus created. Jews and Samaritans rarely, if ever, socialized together. Authentic empowering relationships centered in Jesus Christ tear apart barriers and lead to reconciliation.

Compassionate Forgiveness

In addition to crossing human-made boundaries and creating empowering relationships, Jesus demonstrated the compassionate and forgiving nature of God. As I noted earlier, Jesus regularly shared his mealtime with other people. Scholars call this his "table fellowship."[13] In the first century, if you invited someone to join you at your table, that meant you accepted him or her fully. In fact, the very act of inviting someone over for dinner served as a sign of forgiveness. This must have been overwhelming for those who caught a glimpse of who Jesus really was—God in human flesh. When you received an invitation to Jesus' table, you knew that God had forgiven you. Despite what people said about you, God welcomed you.

On the cross Jesus continued offering forgiveness. He said, "Father, forgive them; for they do not know what they are doing" (Luke 23:34). Consider who Jesus forgave from the cross. First there was Pontius Pilate, who had issued the orders for Jesus' crucifixion. Jesus forgave the one who ordered his crucifixion. Jesus also forgave the Roman soldiers who had beat him, nailed him to the cross, mocked him, and gambled for his clothes. Jesus forgave the religious leaders as well. They proved to be a great disappointment to Jesus, for they did not embrace and support his ministry, but instead convened a mock trial and falsely convicted

Jesus of blasphemy. They led the shouts of "Crucify him," and at the cross they loudly insulted him. Still, Jesus forgave them.

Jesus' pronouncement of forgiveness also included the people who did not show up for his crucifixion—his disciples and his brothers and sisters. In our most difficult moments in life, we want our family and friends to be there for us. Nearly all of Jesus' family and friends were nowhere to be seen. The four Gospels only mention his mother Mary, John of his twelve disciples, and some of the women who had traveled with him (Mary Magdalene, Mary the mother of James and Joses, the mother of James and John, Salome, Mary the wife of Clopas, and others). Jesus forgave those who should have been there for him in his hour of greatest need. Though Jesus was denied and betrayed, abused and abandoned, degraded and debased, convicted and castigated, insulted and injured, he still forgave. Reconciliation calls us to a forgiveness full of compassion and grace.

Many Seeds

What a strange and disturbing sight it must have been for Jesus' followers to see him hanging on the cross. Had not this same Jesus received an angelic choral announcement for his birth? Had not this same Jesus faced off with the devil for forty days and forty nights and come out of the wilderness victorious? Had not this same Jesus given lepers clean skin and brought sight to the blind? Had not this same Jesus calmed storms and walked on water? Had not this same Jesus breathed life back into dead bodies? This same Jesus whose power they had witnessed day after day now hung from a cross.

Jesus' death on the cross appeared to be the end of God's on-site job of reconciliation. Yet Jesus had said a few days earlier, "I tell you the truth, unless a kernel of wheat falls to the ground and dies, it remains only a single seed. But if it dies, it produces many seeds" (John 12:24, NIV). The resurrection of Jesus released the power of reconciliation so that all of us might participate. The ministry of reconciliation was limited as long as Jesus remained in the flesh. In the postresurrection era, however, the power of reconciliation can reach its potential. On-site jobs of reconciliation can occur in multiple locations, simultaneously, through the Spirit of Christ.

We are called to pursue God's one-item agenda of reconciliation. We must cross human-made barriers, create empowering relationships, and embrace compassion-filled forgiveness. We can do this because a single seed fell to the ground on-site in Palestine two thousand years ago. That single seed of reconciliation emerged within the fertile soil of the early church and blossomed into a bountiful first-century harvest. That same seed can produce a harvest of reconciliation in the lives of Jesus' disciples in the twenty-first century.

QUESTIONS FOR DISCUSSION

1. Identify as many boundaries as you can that Jesus crossed in his on-site job of reconciliation. Why did he choose to cross these boundaries? Can you identify any boundaries that he did not or could not cross? If so, what are they?

2. Why is it important to create relationships in the ministry of reconciliation? Recall some personal encounters that illustrate your answer.

3. What are some strategies you use in building relationships? How can these same strategies apply when you attempt to broaden your circle of relationships?

4. What are the limits of your forgiveness at this point in time? What were the limits of Jesus' ability to forgive? How can we grow in our ability to forgive?

5. What about Jesus' ministry of reconciliation most inspires you? Why?

NOTES

1. Samuel Hines, "Nobody with Your Color Eyes Can Be a Preacher," interviewed in William H. Myers, *The Irresistible Urge to Preach: A Collection of African American "Call" Stories* (Atlanta: Aaron Press, 1992), 160, 161.
2. See chapter 7.
3. See Cain Hope Felder, *Troubling Biblical Waters: Race, Class and Family* (Maryknoll, N.Y.: Orbis, 1989), 37; idem, "The Challenges and Implications of Recovering the Afro-Asiatic Identity of Jesus of Nazareth," The BISC Quarterly 4, no. 1 (1993); and Curtiss Paul DeYoung, *Coming Together: The Bible's Message in an Age of Diversity* (Valley Forge, Pa.: Judson, 1995), 8–11, 34–36, 45–47.
4. For a more complete discussion on the inclusiveness of the Scriptures, see DeYoung, *Coming Together,* 1–29, 82–85, 120–50, 155–69; and idem, *Reconciliation: Our Greatest Challenge—Our Only Hope* (Valley Forge, Pa.: Judson, 1997), 43–59.
5. DeYoung, *Coming Together,* 83.
6. Joachim Jeremias, *Jerusalem in the Time of Jesus* (Philadelphia: Fortress, 1969), 353. For more information on Jesus and the Samaritans, see DeYoung, *Coming Together,* 82–84, 124–26.

7. George R. Beasley-Murray, *John,* Word Biblical Commentary vol. 36 (Waco, Tex.: Word, 1987), 62.

8. Ibid.

9. Jeremias, *Jerusalem in the Time of Jesus,* 373, n. 70.

10. Leon Morris, *The Gospel According to John,* The New International Commentary on the New Testament (Grand Rapids: Eerdmans, 1971), 274, n. 68.

11. George R. Beasley-Murray, *John* (Waco, Tex.: Word, 1987), 61.

12. Craig S. Keener, *The IVP Bible Background Commentary: New Testament* (Downers Grove, Ill.: InterVarsity Press, 1993), 272.

13. For more information on "table fellowship," see DeYoung, *Coming Together,* 165–69.

The Church as Agent of Reconciliation

Unity in the Church

Can the Church Rise to the Challenge to Practice Unity?

SAMUEL GEORGE HINES

GOD'S PURPOSE IN THIS WORLD GOES BEYOND THE SAVING OF THE SOULS of men, women, and children, beyond the healing of the sick, and even beyond the liberation of the poor. As I say repeatedly, God's one-item agenda is reconciliation, the bringing of all things together in Jesus Christ. Reconciliation leads to unity. Oneness has nothing to do with whose beliefs are right or whose church traditions are right. Unity finds its center in the heart of God. Are we gathered around Jesus Christ as Lord? Are we involved in living out God's will in the world? Although unity should be the result of pursuing God's agenda of reconciliation, there is no area in which we, the church, have given more room to the world, the devil, and all kinds of contrary forces. We have tried to organize, legalize, and strategize unity, but these methods have not worked. Many of us have become disillusioned with the divisions, the sectarianism, and the denominationalism in the church. We have been unable to accomplish any kind of basic unity either inside or outside the church. We pursue our separate agendas and scoff at those who do not think and act like we do.

An unbreakable connection exists between unity, reconciliation, for-giveness, repentance, and evangelism. Certainly, a large part of our fail-ures in evangelism come because we try to evangelize among groups and in communities when we have no bridges to link us with the needy people or with other persons who, by the will of God, are also God's ambassadors. We need to make the effort and take the time to network with others in order to present a united witness to the world. In spite of all the organizations—the National Council of Churches, the World Council of Churches, the National Association of Evangelicals, the Christian Holiness Association, and other ecumenical associations—we still have not properly understood, and certainly have not achieved, any full measure of unity. We fail because we do not understand that the heart of true unity centers in the person of Jesus Christ and not in a program or organization. Jesus expressed his desire for unity in his final days on this earth when he prayed:

> As you have sent me into the world, so I have sent them into the world. And for their sakes I sanctify myself, so that they also may be sanctified in truth.
>
> I ask not only on behalf of these, but also on behalf of those who will believe in me through their word, that they may all be one. As you, Father, are in me and I am in you, may they also may be in us, so that the world may believe that you have sent me. The glory that you have given me I have given them, so that they may be one, as we are one. (John 17:18–22)

Unity Is Not Uniformity

Uniformity of doctrine or coming together under one form of church government cannot produce unity. The unity of the church emerges through the organic unity of the people constituted spiritually as the body of Christ. That unity springs forth from Christ's name, person, will, ministry, work, and function in the world. Doctrine and culture too often divide, but Christ unites. In our attempt to achieve organizational unity through mergers, councils, and conclaves, we have left out the need for the radical action of reconciliation. Therefore, our attempts fail because unity cannot come about without a reconciliation grounded in our total love for God and our mutual love for each other. Jesus said that our most important tool for evangelism would be our love for each other. He said: "I give you a new commandment, that you love one another. Just as I have loved you, you also should love one another. By this everyone will know that you are my disciples, if you have love for one another" (John 13:34–35).

Acknowledge the Effects of Sin

In order to live in unity, we must open our eyes to the effects of sin. Sin causes polarization and alienation and estranges people from one another. Sin is spiritual apartheid that forces us apart from God and from one another. There can be no restoration without going through reconciliation. As I said earlier, the New Testament verb most often translated *reconciliation* means "radical change." Reconciliation means changing status, position, and relationships. Reconciliation is a *heart* change. Radical change is indispensable for a sinner who desires to fit back into relationship with God. Similar radical change is also necessary for people—even redeemed people—to fit back into proper relationships with one another.

An eye-opening example for me came on a trip to South Africa where whites and blacks, who had long been estranged under their system of political apartheid, sought reconciliation. And they found it. Why? Because of real repentance and forgiveness. Real contrition occurred. People cried penitently before one another saying, "I have wronged you. Can I get forgiveness from you? Can you tell me what I need to do to make things right with you?" This event happened in 1983 when four Americans and I attended the National Initiative on Reconciliation held near Petermaritsburg. We had a wonderful session confessing our sins and discussing ways of dealing with apartheid. Hearts were broken. Afrikaners from the Dutch Reformed Church, English-speaking whites, coloreds, Indians, and blacks (who had come from many different tribes) were all there together, and God worked out some marvelous things.

A spirit of penitence came over the group when a leading Afrikaner minister of the Dutch Reformed Church stood up, sobbing, and asked for a hearing. He told the group that in his fifty years of living in South Africa he had never before understood the black man's cry. He had heard about it, but he had never heard it with his own ears. He confessed how ashamed and grieved he felt that such inhumane things had been done to human beings. He then proceeded to publicly repent on behalf of white South Africans and to ask forgiveness of blacks. He abjectly declared that he did not at that point know how or when things would be set right, but he asked again for forgiveness and that his people be given a chance to take the steps that must be made *together.*

A black Presbyterian minister, who had become a friend of mine over the years, sat beside me. He turned to me and said, "Sam, pinch me. I want to know if I am really in South Africa, hearing what I am hearing." Since the meeting had become a confession period, the time came for the black community to speak their word for reconciliation. One black minister rose and expressed his remorse by declaring that he repented of the fact that his people had been foolish enough to let the white people sit on their necks all these years. A noted black anti-apartheid leader stood up and addressed his minister friend as a loved brother who had supported him and worked hard to bring change in the policies of the nation. He reminded the brother that this was not one of their protest meetings, but a time for repentance and forgiveness. His words made the difference between integration and reconciliation very clear.

Until we ask for forgiveness and recognize the sin that causes disunity and estrangement—even between Christian brothers and sisters—all of our ideals of unity are dreams that will never come to pass. The church must insist on reconciliation and not settle for lesser goals like integration, accommodation, and tolerance. These are counterfeits of reconciliation and will not bring about real unity. Any godly movement toward reconciliation must be radical and call people to do something that they cannot do without God's supernatural help. As God's church we must take a look at ourselves and say, "Where are we in this whole business of unity?" Many people make unity their banner and reconciliation from secular viewpoints their emphasis. We need to lead the way in God's great movement to reconcile people. The church, the body of Christ, is uniquely significant in carrying out God's one-item agenda. It is primarily in the church that the union between God and human beings is most regularly proclaimed, confessed, and realized and it is through the church that godly precepts and principles can be most readily taught and modeled.

The Manifestation of Unity

Unity in the church becomes possible when we move beyond rhetoric to practice. The apostle Paul believed that unity was manifested when we demonstrate a willingness to make specific commitments in our lives. He wrote in his letter to the church in Ephesus, "I therefore, the prisoner in the Lord, beg you to lead a life worthy of the calling to which you have been called" (4:1). Paul then outlined how to promote unity in the church—"with all humility and gentleness, with patience, bearing with one another in love, making every effort to maintain the unity of the Spirit in the bond of peace" (Ephesians 4:2,3).

The first manifestation of unity is humility. Bigotry is the opposite of humility. Prejudice indicates foolish pride. Whenever we adopt a frame of mind that causes us to set ourselves up as the ultimate measure for living, we lapse into bigotry. Pride and arrogance separate us from other people. Conceit and bigotry make us keep our brothers and sisters at arm's length. When we keep our own unworthiness constantly in mind, we have neither time nor room in our thinking to indulge in or hold on to foolish pride. We must allow the Holy Spirit to so transform us that we develop a spirit of genuine humility rather than fall prey to prejudice.

The second thing the apostle mentioned was gentleness. One aspect of gentleness is to remain teachable. I have heard people say, in so many words or by their body language, "I don't mind having fellowship with those people, but they have nothing to teach me. If they will listen to me, fine, but they have nothing of worth to tell me." When we exhibit such an attitude, we reveal our own ignorance of particular areas in our lives that need instruction. The author of Hebrews wrote that Jesus "learned obedience through what he suffered" (5:8). This suggests that gentleness may also be seen in the inner strength to endure pain while obeying God's direction.

Certainly gentleness means having the ability to control anger. It takes a large and strong spirit to be gentle while dealing with others who frustrate, irritate, and sometimes seek to annihilate us, if not with arms at least with words. Remember what Jesus said to Roman governor Pilate when he declared that he had the power to take away Jesus' life. Jesus said, "You would have no power over me unless it had been given you from above" (John 19:11). This is the sequel to his words to the disciples when he told them, "I lay down my life for the sheep. . . . No one takes it from me, but I lay it down of my own accord. I have power to lay it down, and I have power to take it up again . . ." (John 10:15,18). It takes unusual and supernatural strength to be gentle.

Another area the apostle Paul pointed out in which we have to work if we desire to manifest unity is the need to develop sensitivity to other people. He mentioned the two-sided coinage of this sensitivity— patience and "bearing with one another in love" (Ephesians 4:2). There are few things that can disrupt unity like impatience does. We must not set a timetable for someone else's spiritual development. If we are going to be a unifying force with people, we must have patience. Our timetable for a person or a group may differ from God's plan and disrupt unity. Patience never gives in to defeat and never gives up on a brother or a sister.

Bearing with one another in love is not tolerance. No one wants to be a victim of mere tolerance. Putting up with people is no way to achieve unity. This kind of attitude communicates, in intangible ways, our ultimate resistance to the call of God. No unity of spirit can be forged in this type of atmosphere. There has to be a bearing together in love. It is literally getting under the load together and bearing with the other person as if their burden were our burden. It is developing and expressing a loving attitude that is determined to seek the welfare of the other person. The Amplified Bible interprets bearing one another in love as meaning: "Making allowances because you love one another."

The next manifestation of unity that Paul highlighted was "making every effort to maintain the unity of the Spirit in the bond of peace" (Ephesians 4:3). The unity of the Spirit is an inside job, which only God can accomplish through the Holy Spirit. Paul informed the saints in Ephesus that they have to keep this unity "in the bond of peace," which is the external evidence that manifests the work of the Spirit within us. This kind of peaceful spirit should always be a hallmark of the people of God if relationships are kept right. Differences of ideas will arise and diversities of temperament will exist, but the people of God can live together in peace when the Holy Spirit is in control of their lives. Unity becomes manifested in the church when we practice humility, gentleness, and patience in conjunction with love and a peaceful spirit.

Unity Means Commitment to Jesus Christ

To maintain unity means making a decision to be committed to living out God's agenda. God does not tell us to make ourselves united. God tells us to keep the unity already accomplished in Jesus Christ. Keeping the unity of the faith requires commitment. Commitment is more than good feelings. We must decide to meet face-to-face and link arms with our brothers and sisters. The only people who can unite *in* Christ are people who commit *to* Christ. The only people who can truly unite in ministry and mission are people who commit to the goal that Christ made his own. That goal is doing the will of God. Each person fills his or her own place in the body through a willingness to make oneself available to Christ and therefore to the rest of the body in the same way that the hand brings its abilities to the body. The hand is not only available to the hand; the hand is available to the whole body. That is the kind of commitment that will keep us united. The apostle Paul told believers in Rome that "we are members one of another" (Romans 12:5).

One of the main deterrents to keeping unity is our differing doctrinal perspectives, our different understandings of what certain Bible passages mean. We bring differing perceptions from our history and environment. I am talking about how people respond to the truth. Many different things influence our encounter with truth. While the revelation is usually the same, our interpretation can differ. Danger alarms should sound when any group falls into the rut of believing they possess "the whole truth." Our doctrines must remain progressive as we search the Scriptures and as we are led by the Holy Spirit to pursue those paths where the challenge of truth may lead us. If we ever feel that we have "the whole truth," then we have closed the road that pursues the truth. We may have good friends whose eschatological views (the teaching about the end of time) differ from ours, but we can still feel close kinship with those friends. We may have good friends whose views of the doctrine of church government differ from ours, but that should not prevent us from being very close to them in ministry and mission. We can respect each other from our positions and understandings.

What are the key beliefs? We must stand firm upon some points. For instance, if someone did not believe that Jesus Christ is Lord, I could not begin to have Christian communion with that person, because Jesus is my basis of communion with God. If someone rejected the divinity of Jesus, I would have problems walking jointly with her or him; that does not mean, however, that I could not do anything with that person. The keystone of the church is Jesus the Christ. On that we must agree. We may debate other doctrines, but we must not allow anyone to destroy or break our fellowship with Jesus.

The Foundation of Unity

According to the apostle Paul, the unity of believers in Christ was built on the foundation that, "There is one body and one Spirit, just as you were called to the one hope of your calling, one Lord, one faith, one baptism, one God and Father of all, who is above all and through all and in all" (Ephesians 4:4–6). "One body" is a very strong biblical concept implying a united church of which Jesus Christ is the head. There is one head and one body—not one head and many bodies or one body with many heads. No matter where believers in Jesus are located or what label they may wear, they all come under the headship of Jesus Christ. As Christians, if anyone should ask us, "To what body do you belong?" our answer should be "The body of Christ." We should never confuse or name a denomination, group, or movement as "the body."

A body without a spirit is a corpse. So Paul wrote that the body of Christ was made alive, animated and quickened by one Spirit. There is not a distinct spirit for different members of the body because they wear various labels, belong to differing denominations, or worship in diverse ways. Human reasoning may lead us to slant our interpretations of God in different directions, but the one Holy Spirit will ultimately "guide us into all truth" (John 16:13).

The apostle Paul made it clear that for a disciple of Jesus Christ, there is only one hope of our calling. Even though Christians may not see eye-to-eye on every issue, all believers are going toward one destiny. There is one end in view for the whole church. Some catch the vision earlier than others. Some see it more clearly and comprehend some of its mysteries more readily than others. Some are more excited about what they understand than others are, but there is only one single hope for all who trust in Jesus. It is the hope of the final consummation of the purposes of God in a perfected community of believers who are progressively maturing and conforming to the image of Jesus Christ. So, just as we are one body with one Spirit, we have one hope.

Included in the foundation of the unity of church is that there is only one Lord—one sovereign for all believers. Paul declared that no individual is able to claim Jesus Christ as Lord but by the Holy Spirit. The believer is a person who has come to the conclusion that, in spite of all that is happening above, around, and within us—in spite of all the explorations in space and developments in cyberspace, all the upheavals, all the violence and immorality in our world—there is still just one Lord, one master of the universe and all in it, and that is Jesus Christ.

The foundation of one faith causes much difficulty within the body of Christ. The problem usually surrounds our misapplication of the word "faith." Many take this to mean a system of doctrines or a creed (written or unwritten). That kind of thinking makes it almost impossible for people to accommodate any interpretation of Scripture that differs from their own, which will invariably lead to division. The apostle did not write that there is one creed or one system of church management or one style of worship; he said that there is one faith. There is a unique and intrinsic link between God and human beings. Wherever Christians are found, regardless of their brand of religion, they are part of the same body of Christ, the church, with the same Spirit, the same hope, and the same unshakable assurance that Jesus Christ is Lord. This is the faith—that Jesus is the Son of God! He was dead, but he has risen and is reigning with redeeming power in the lives of his people.

Many Christians also find one baptism to be a problematic concept in the foundation of unity. A young man once said to me that he had been baptized as a very young person and afterward, he became a Christian. He sincerely questioned whether he should be baptized again because, he said, "The Bible says we have 'one baptism.'" Paul found some believers in Ephesus who said that they had been baptized with John's baptism—the baptism of repentance (Acts 19:1–7). After hearing the gospel about Jesus, as preached by Paul, they were baptized again. This second baptism was in the name of the Lord Jesus. When Paul stated in his letter to the church at Ephesus that there is one baptism, he was not speaking of a physical baptism. Paul was saying that there is one installation experience when a believer is immersed into the life of Christ. It is a spiritual baptism. "For in the one Spirit we were all baptized into one body—Jews or Greeks, slaves or free—and we were all made to drink of one Spirit" (1 Corinthians 12:13). When we have had this spiritual immersion, we live according to the dictates of the Holy Spirit. The real question is not what style of baptism or how many times we have been baptized, but whether we have had a spiritual immersion. Are we still immersed in the ways, mores, and thinking of the world, or have we been baptized by the Holy Spirit?

Like Jesus, Paul taught that the only ultimate reality is the one, eternal God of the universe. The whole issue of life boils down to this one reality—there is only "one God and Father of all, who is above all and through all and in all" (Ephesians 4:6). If we have anything good within us, it is there because God put it there. If there is anything worthwhile and lasting happening through us, it is the one sovereign God who permits it to be accomplished. On the basis of the truth that one almighty God rules us all, and on the foundation of our hope, faith, and baptism in the Spirit of Jesus, there is a glorious unity among believers in the church, the body of Jesus Christ.

Conclusion

When we leave the theoretical and come to deal with the practical, we realize that we live in a terrible age of separation. We need to do something quickly and effectively to lift up the message of the kingdom of God that points us to unity in diversity. Given how many people claim to be born-again, Spirit-filled believers, we should have a greater impact on society. We, as the church, are not significantly changing our world. We do not even challenge society as we should! We misunderstand what it means to be a powerful church. We are obsessed with grabbing for power—in politics and in industry, as well as in the church. While we need Christians in politics and everywhere else, we must never allow power to become our number-one priority.

We read in John 13 that when Jesus' hour had come, when he knew that all things were given into his hand, he did not grab power. He grabbed a basin and a towel and washed the feet of his disciples. Jesus declared that his kingdom was not of this world. Unity comes through reconciling action. We must be about the business of "washing" our brothers' and sisters' feet, for we see power, not on the throne, but at our neighbors' feet. The church has that message. Let us acknowledge our own sin and failure to declare the message of reconciliation and unity and practice it the way God wants us to. Our fears must not be stronger than our love for one another, for we have a mandate to be ambassadors of reconciliation. We will fulfill that mandate when our love for God and one another grows stronger and finds its power at the feet of others.

> As the Father has loved me, so I have loved you; abide in my love. If you keep my commandments, you will abide in my love, just as I have kept my Father's commandments and abide in his love. (John 15:9–10)

QUESTIONS FOR DISCUSSION

1. Describe a time when you experienced unity in the church. What made that possible? How did it feel?

2. Do you believe that the church will ever be united? Why or why not?

3. Identify the difference between unity and uniformity. How can unity be achieved without uniformity?

4. In what ways do sin and the lack of forgiveness and repentance impede unity?

5. Why is the story of Jesus washing his disciples' feet such a powerful image for unity and reconciliation?

4

A First-Century Church for the Twenty-first Century

Lessons Learned from the First-Century Church Regarding Reconciliation

CURTISS PAUL DEYOUNG

LOS ANGELES EXPERIENCED A BRIEF GLIMPSE OF THE POSSIBILITY OF reconciliation in the church during the first decade of the twentieth century. William J. Seymour began preaching during April 1906 (Holy Week) on Azusa Street. The "Azusa Street Revival" continued without break for three years and attracted thousands of people from diverse backgrounds of race, socioeconomic class, and culture. For a short period of time, the first-century church seemed to make an appearance in the twentieth century. Seymour described the event: "Multitudes have come. God makes no difference in nationality; Ethiopians, Chinese, Indians, Mexicans, and other nationalities worship together."[1] According to Christian ethicist and pastor Cheryl Sanders, "Seymour believed that the revival itself was a sign of divine approbation of racial unity."[2]

William Seymour's preaching was informed by his theological commitment to the marriage of holiness and unity that he had discovered in the Holiness Movement, particularly in the Church of God (Anderson, Indiana), where he was a minister.[3] Seymour, an African American, shared leadership in the revival with individuals of other races. He also welcomed women in leadership roles. Richard Foster describes this event as "an all-inclusive fellowship" that was meant "to break racial,

gender, and nationalistic barriers and offer the world a historic opportunity for genuine healing and reconciliation."[4]

Unfortunately, the Azusa Street Revival began to unravel when some
white Christian leaders quietly left, uncomfortable with the multicultural
nature of the group. Other white Christian leaders spoke openly against
the idea of interracial community. One such leader, Charles Parham, dra-
matically declared his distaste for racial reconciliation: "God is sick at his
stomach!"[5] Eight years after the beginning of the revival, the congregation led by Seymour at Azusa Street gathered on Sundays as a "local black
church with an occasional white visitor."[6] Prejudice reared its ugly head,
and the leaders of the Azusa Street Revival could not sustain this Spirit-
inspired experiment of first-century Christian community.

In the prologue to section 2, Dr. Hines reminds us of the challenge
we face in living out unity and reconciliation in the church. The Azusa
Street Revival suggests that even in the midst of a strong witness to reconciliation, the fires of unity can be quenched. We may even question
the possibility of such an occurrence. Certainly we can point to the
ministry of Jesus—as I did in chapter 3—as an example of how to live
this call to reconciliation. Yet we can counter with the assertion that we
do not carry the divine nature of Jesus Christ. In this chapter I examine
the process of reconciliation in the early church, as described in the
Acts of the Apostles. Perhaps their first-century narrative can inform
and impact the story of the church that will be written in the twenty-
first century.

Reconciliation Is God's Will

The first-century church began as a group of about 120 people who
shared a commitment to live according to the teachings and example of
Jesus Christ. The community of believers included the Twelve (minus
Judas), the women who followed Jesus as disciples, Mary the mother of
Jesus, and his blood brothers (Acts 1:13–15). On the day of Pentecost
they received the empowerment and anointing of the Holy Spirit in a
rather spectacular fashion, after which they preached to a crowd that
included people residing in Jerusalem, broader Palestine, and Arabia,
but also many from places located on the continents we today call Asia,
Africa, and Europe (2:9–11). According to the author of Acts, on that
day about 3,000 additional people joined the life of the early community of believers. Soon this original group of 120 expanded even further

to 5,000 (4:4). Acts described these 5,000 or more believers in Jerusalem as "of one heart and soul" (4:32). A powerful witness to reconciliation must have been occurring in the Jerusalem church.

This community of the reconciled nurtured and sustained their faith through a discipline that included the apostles' teaching, fellowship, the breaking of bread, and prayer (2:42). The church in Jerusalem experienced boldness in their witness and miracles in their daily lives as a result of this devotion to God. One of the miracles was an amazing economic reconciliation.

> All who believed were together and had all things in common; they would sell their possessions and goods and distribute the proceeds to all, as any had need. . . . Now the whole group of those who believed were of one heart and soul, and no one claimed private ownership of any possessions, but everything they owned was held in common. . . . There was not a needy person among them, for as many as owned lands or houses sold them and brought the proceeds of what was sold. They laid it at the apostles' feet, and it was distributed to each as any had need. (2:44–45; 4:32,34–35)

Although the Jerusalem church had embraced this powerful model of reconciliation, its ministry did not move outside of Jerusalem. In Acts 1:8 the last words Jesus spoke were: "But you will receive power when the Holy Spirit has come upon you; and you will be my witnesses in Jerusalem, in all Judea and Samaria, and to the ends of the earth." Despite this commission from Jesus, they stayed in Jerusalem. Everything changed when the religious leaders (and Saul) unleashed persecution on the church after the death of Stephen, one of the Seven (6:5,8–15; 7:1–8:3). The author of Acts declares that "all except the apostles were scattered throughout the countryside of Judea and Samaria," and "those who were scattered went from place to place, proclaiming the word" (8:1,4). The church did not run from persecution. They preached as they scattered. Jesus' commission was pursued as a result of suffering.

Philip, also one of the Seven, went into Samaria and started preaching the word (8:4–25). A great revival occurred in Samaria. We read in Acts that "when the apostles at Jerusalem heard that Samaria had accepted the word of God, they sent Peter and John to them" (8:14). In some denominations, when something happens out in the field, headquarters sends someone to make sure that what has occurred accords with the beliefs and practices promoted by the center of operations. Peter and John were sent by the church in Jerusalem to discover the legitimacy of the revival in Samaria. Despite the numerous times that Jesus ministered in Samaria, there may have been a residue of prejudice among the Jerusalem believers. Peter and John discovered a vibrant movement of God. So they prayed for the Samaritan people who had gathered, and the Holy Spirit came in the same fashion as in Jerusalem. The last time John had been in Samaria, he and his brother, James, asked Jesus to call down fire on Samaria (Luke 9:51–56). Perhaps John needed to see the power of the Holy Spirit operate in the lives of Samaritans before some of his prejudice could be overcome. What a gift of reconciliation for those in Samaria who had heard that John and James had asked Jesus to call down fire on a Samaritan village!

There was now a church in Jerusalem and a church in Samaria. Let's apply some imagination to the text. The Jerusalem church did not experience integration because of this evangelistic effort; the Samaritans would remain in Samaria with their own congregation. This factor does not appear in the Bible, and you may disagree with the imaginative approach I am taking, but knowing our flawed humanity and struggle with prejudice, there may have been some comfort in this separation. Thus, there was a Jerusalem church and a Samaritan church.

As Philip continued witnessing to the power of the resurrection of Christ, the Holy Spirit directed him to share this message with an Ethiopian traveling down the Gaza Road from Jerusalem to Africa (Acts 8:26–40). He served as the chief financial officer for the empire of Queen Candice, the great kingdom of Nubia (biblical Ethiopia), which is today the Sudan.[7] When Philip arrived, he heard the Ethiopian official reading from the scroll of Isaiah in his chariot. Given he could read, owned a scroll (although not a Jew), and rode in a chariot, he held high social status. When Philip shared the word with him, the official embraced Christ. No one from Jerusalem arrived to authenticate this conversion. Since the treasury official was on his way back home to Africa, it is possible that we now had an Ethiopian church, as well as a Jerusalem church and a Samaritan church.

Then an event occurred that stretched the limits of the early church's understanding of inclusiveness (Acts 10:1–11:18). The apostle Peter received a vision from God in which God said, "What God has made clean, you must not call profane" (10:15). After the vision, the Holy Spirit prompted him to go to the house of a Roman centurion named Cornelius living in Caesarea. This request was not easy for Peter to obey, because when Peter entered the home of a Gentile, he would lose his ritual purity. Further, this was the home of a Roman Gentile, and the Jews were under the oppressive colonial rule of Rome. Even the name of the city where Cornelius resided—Caesarea—served as a reminder of Caesar's reign. As a Roman military officer, Cornelius enforced the oppression mandated by Rome. Thus, Peter required a vision from God to enter Cornelius's house. He obeyed the vision and preached to Cornelius and his entire household. As a result, the Holy Spirit fell upon them in the same fashion that the Spirit had fallen upon the 120 in the upper room on the day of Pentecost (11:15).

The Jerusalem church did not send representatives to Caesarea. Rather, they called Peter back to headquarters to give an account of his actions in this Roman centurion's house. Peter explained to the leaders of the church in Jerusalem what happened there:

> "As I began to speak, the Holy Spirit came on them as he had come on us at the beginning. Then I remembered what the Lord had said: 'John baptized with water, but you will be baptized with the Holy Spirit.' So if God gave them the same gift as he gave us, who believed in the Lord Jesus Christ, who was I to think that I could oppose God?"
>
> When they heard this, they had no further objections and praised God, saying, "So then, God has granted even the Gentiles repentance unto life" (11:15–18, NIV).

Once the Jerusalem believers heard that the Holy Spirit had visited Cornelius and his household in the same way he had visited them at Pentecost, they accepted the conversion of Romans as God's will. William Seymour once said, "I can say through the power of the Spirit, that wherever God can get a people that will come together in one accord and one mind in the Word of God, the baptism of the Holy Spirit will fall on them, like as at Cornelius' house."[8] So we now had a Jerusalem church, a Samaritan church, an Ethiopian church, and a Roman house church.

Philip and Peter were not the only people expanding the mission of the early church after the martyrdom of Stephen. Disciples from Cyprus and Cyrene also spread the reconciling message of a resurrected Christ. We read in Acts:

> Now those who were scattered because of the persecution that took place over Stephen traveled as far as Phoenicia, Cyprus, and Antioch, and they spoke the word to no one except Jews. But among them were some men

of Cyprus and Cyrene who, on coming to Antioch, spoke to the Hellenists (Greeks) also, proclaiming the Lord Jesus. The hand of the Lord was with them, and a great number became believers and turned to the Lord. (11:19–21)

In Antioch, the believers reached out for the first time to both Jews and Greeks, creating the first multicultural congregation.

The alarm bells must have rung loudly at headquarters! Acts states, "News of this came to the ears of the church in Jerusalem, and they sent Barnabas to Antioch" (11:22). News traveled quickly, and the Jerusalem church sent Barnabas. (Perhaps they had given up on Peter.) Barnabas encouraged the new disciples in Antioch, and the congregation flourished (11:23–24). Upon discovering the unique challenges of a cross-cultural ministry, Barnabas went to Tarsus and found Saul (Paul) to serve as a ministry partner (11:25–26), for Saul was both a Jew and a Roman citizen. Together they provided leadership for an entire year, and "it was in Antioch that the disciples were first called 'Christians'" (11:26).

According to the depiction of the early church in the book of Acts, the influence of the church in Jerusalem waned as the church in Antioch took center stage. Samuel Hines wrote: "Notice what happened at Antioch: When the evangelists began preaching to everyone, all kinds of people entered the life of that church—all kinds of races and nationalities, all kinds of vocations and social classes. God chose the church at Antioch, therefore, to be the beginning of the missionary movement."[9] As the church in Antioch sent forth Saul, Barnabas, and others (13:2ff.), they took the Antioch model of church with them. They added to the powerful model developed in Jerusalem a broader multicultural vision. The Holy Spirit who empowers our efforts today is the same Holy Spirit that visited Jerusalem, Samaria, an Ethiopian official, a Roman house, and Antioch in the first century. We must embrace the ministry of reconciliation as God's will for the twenty-first century.

Reconciliation Is Sustained through Creative Partnerships

Given the difficulties of sustaining multicultural outreaches like the Azusa Street Revival, we must ask, How did the church in Antioch sustain a multicultural, reconciling fellowship? Acts states, "Now in the church at Antioch there were prophets and teachers: Barnabas, Simeon who was called Niger, Lucius of Cyrene, Manaen a member of the court of Herod the ruler, and Saul" (13:1). A creative multicultural partnership of leaders guided the congregation of believers in Antioch. The early church must have learned this principle of team leadership from Jesus' ministry. Since Jesus was God in human flesh, he could have done his ministry all by himself. Jesus did not need help. Yet he chose twelve disciples (Luke 6:12–16), a group of women (Luke 8:1–4), and seventy-two others (Luke 10:1) to serve on his ministry team. Jesus empowered others through creative ministry partnerships.

The apostle Paul consistently preached the gospel through the use of ministry partnerships. Paul and Barnabas served together in Antioch and then traveled together in ministry (Acts 13:2–15:35). The book of Acts notes that Paul served in partnership with Silas (15:40ff.), Timothy (16:1ff.), Priscilla and Aquila (18:1–26), Erastus (19:22), Sopator (20:4), Aristarchus (20:4), Secundus (20:4), Gaius (20:4), Tychicus (20:4), Trophimus (20:4; 21:29), and many others. Given the many uses of "we" in the text, the author of Acts (many believe this was Luke) also served as a ministry partner. In the final chapter of his letter to the Romans, Paul listed thirty-four of his partners in ministry by name (16:1–15), sixteen of whom were women. Paul was comfortable with partnerships between men and women in ministry. In many of his letters, he mentioned ministry partners who joined him at the location where he composed his letter, or in some cases, who helped in the writing of the letter.

Leadership teams and a spirit of partnership sustain the ministry of reconciliation. Samuel Hines illustrates this in chapter 6 when he speaks of his life partner—his wife, Dalineta, and his covenant partners. He also describes broader partnerships of pastoral leaders with lay leaders and of urban congregations with suburban congregations. After we have decided to embrace the ministry of reconciliation as God's will, we sustain this ministry through developing creative partnerships, first with God as our ultimate partner and then with others who have complementary callings.

Reconciliation Is Safeguarded through Courageous and Bold Responses

Anyone who has sought to be faithful to God's call to be an ambassador of reconciliation knows that this ministry is fraught with challenges. The apostle Paul wrote about an incident that had the potential to destroy the vibrant witness to reconciliation in the Antioch church (Galatians 2:11–21). Paul said that the apostle Peter visited the Antioch church. Perhaps he was there on a teaching or preaching mission. Initially, Peter seemed comfortable in this congregation that brought together believers of Jewish ancestry with Christians of so many other ethnic identities. He ate at the same table with believers of differing ethnic groups—a continuation of the table fellowship of Jesus I discussed in chapter 3. A group from the "circumcision" group arrived in Antioch teaching that Gentiles must first become Jews before they could be accepted as Christians. They expected one to keep all the purity rules, such as not eating at the same table with Gentiles. Under pressure from the circumcision group, Peter compromised the reconciliation witness and began eating only with the Jews in the church. When a leader falls prey to prejudice, many others will follow. Barnabas, the man who nurtured this church from its earliest years, followed Peter in this compromise. The church at Antioch began to split internally along ethnic lines.

Paul was outraged by what happened. He could not accept that Peter, the one who saw a vision about God's desire to include Gentiles in the church, could act in a way that would lead to a split in the church. Thus, he confronted Peter. If you read the text in Galatians closely, Paul did not shame Peter. He said, in essence, "Peter, you and I have the same faith, you and I follow the same Christ, and you know this is wrong." We need to be aware that everything we have worked for in reconciliation is fragile and has the potential to fall apart. We need to prepare for the possibility of setbacks and sabotage in our efforts at building unity. And we must safeguard our progress in reconciliation through much prayer, and perhaps, like Paul, provide a courageous and bold response.

Reconciliation Is Possible When God's People Are Transformed

The first-century church understood reconciliation as God's will, sustained it through partnerships, and safeguarded it with bold action. They also recognized that reconciliation becomes possible only when we have been transformed by the same message we preach. Personal transformation precedes the practice of reconciliation. We must experience healing before we can reach out to others with the message of healing. We must be reconciled with God through Jesus Christ before we can witness to the good news of God's reconciling love. To gain a fuller understanding of what it means to be transformed, we will here examine the process of transformation that occurred among the leaders at Antioch.

The apostle Peter, while not one of the five ministry team leaders at Antioch, participated in the life of the Antioch church (as noted above) and played a significant part in the development of the first-century church. The transformation that occurred in Peter's life was significant and ongoing. A deeply rooted struggle with prejudice and perhaps rage provided Peter with his greatest challenge. Like some Palestinian Jews, Peter may have entertained strong feelings of bitterness and hatred toward Romans in particular and bigotry toward Gentiles in general. So after ministering with Jesus for three years and preaching the sermon at Pentecost, Peter still required a vision from God to enter Cornelius's house. At the Roman centurion's house Peter testified to a new understanding, "I truly understand that God shows no partiality, but in every nation anyone who fears him and does what is right is acceptable to him" (Acts 10:34–35). Then he witnessed the Holy Spirit come upon this gathering of Romans in the same way as he had experienced the Spirit in Jerusalem.

Yet Peter's choices contributed to ethnic division at the Antioch church. The process of his personal transformation remained incomplete. If we are honest with ourselves, we may find that there are ways we can relate to Peter. Reconciliation is an ongoing process. Through self-examination we may discover that God has more work to accomplish in our lives. We can remain hopeful. If tradition is correct, Peter's last years were spent ministering in Rome.[10] He had finally been so transformed by the love of God that he could love his enemies. Reconciliation proved possible in Antioch because Peter met a Jesus who invited him to let go of anger and prejudice and love his enemies.

In addition to Peter, Simeon and Lucius served as leaders at the Antioch church. Simeon was called Niger, which means black. According to biblical scholar Craig Keener, his nickname, Niger, may have indicated that he had a dark complexion and was from Africa.[11] Lucius was from Cyrene in North Africa, now called Libya. If these two men both came from Africa, then Antioch was a long way from their homes. Perhaps Simeon and Lucius had left the comfort of a familiar place to minister in Antioch. To leave our comfort zone to follow God requires that we experience a transformation. Perhaps as we step out in faith, the transformation occurs. Something amazing happens as we stretch our comfort zone.

In 1981, at age twenty-three, I moved to New York City to work for a year at a shelter for runaway youth in Times Square called Covenant House. I was born in a rural area, raised in a suburban environment, and yet felt called to serve God in the heart of the largest city in the United States. I stepped out of my comfort zone in many ways. First, I did not know anyone in New York. Second, I was working with young people who were experiencing the tragic consequences of life on the street. Little in my twenty-three years of life had prepared me for this work. Third, I was living in a lay Franciscan Catholic community where I attended mass daily and chanted the Psalms as a part of three hours of daily prayer. Not only was I raised a Protestant (Church of God) and in a Protestant town (Dutch Reformed Kalamazoo, Michigan), but I wondered if Roman Catholics could even be Christians. The life witness to Christ of the individuals in this community put my doubts to rest and challenged my own understanding of faith. Shortly after arriving in New York City, I awakened one day to the awareness that I was completely out of my comfort zone—twenty-four hours a day, seven days a week—and became overwhelmed by feelings of culture shock, loneliness, and helplessness.

In an attempt to counter feeling like an outsider, I decided to visit a congregation of my own denomination. At least I could enjoy familiar worship and fellowship. One Sunday morning I took the subway to the northern section of Manhattan in New York City. Oblivious to the location of my destination, I arrived in Harlem, a cultural mecca for African Americans in the United States. When I walked through the doors of the church building, I was the first white person to visit there in years. Once again I found myself out of my comfort zone.

I had felt completely out of my comfort zone when I arrived in New York City. I had followed the lead of God and traveled to an unfamiliar place with no guarantee of the outcome. Yet by the end of that year, in many of the places where I originally experienced discomfort, I felt a greater sense of comfort. I fully embraced life in a large city. I felt at home in a Catholic community. I gained confidence counseling runaway youth. And I served as an associate minister, preaching regularly, at the church in Harlem. My comfort zone had expanded. Like Lucius and Simeon, when God's reconciling power transforms us, we constantly stretch our comfort zone. Reconciliation was possible in Antioch because Simeon and Lucius met a Jesus who invited them to let go of comfort and encounter the blessing of ministry.

Another leader in Antioch was Manaen. Only Acts notes his involvement. All that can be known about him is that he "had been brought up with Herod the tetrarch" (13:1, NIV). Craig Keener writes:

That Manaen was "brought up" with Herod may mean they had the same wet nurse. Slaves who grew up in the master's household with the son who would inherit them were often later freed by the son, who had been a companion at play; even as slaves they were powerful because of their relationship to the owner. . . . Especially in Greek culture, friendships from youth determined political alliances and favors. Thus, until the fall of Herod Antipas ("the tetrarch") perhaps a decade before, Manaen had held a socially prominent position.[12]

Whether Manaen was a freed slave or a foster brother to Herod, he could benefit from his status as a political insider. He had access to power and prestige.

Manaen let go of his power and privilege to be a part of the church. Our society places a lot of emphasis on gaining "insider" status, yet the goal of being an insider often directly contradicts the faith modeled by Jesus. Transformation comes when we place a higher value on being an insider with God than with the human powers that be. Manaen's choice to serve God in Antioch can only be explained through a personal transformation. Reconciliation was possible in Antioch because Manaen met a Jesus who invited him to let go of political power and embrace Holy Spirit power.

Barnabas also provided leadership at the Antioch church. Born and raised a Levite from Cyprus named Joseph, he was renamed Barnabas ("son of encouragement or refreshment") by the apostles in Jerusalem (4:36–37). He was an affluent landowner who sold some of his property and brought the money to the apostles to distribute to those in need. In the process, Barnabas let go of some of the economic comfort and privilege that came from owning land. In our day with so much pressure to prosper financially, this act by Barnabas seems ill conceived. We often place more trust for our security in the stock market than in the God of the universe. Reconciliation was possible in Antioch because Barnabas met a Jesus who invited him to let go of economic security so he could enjoy the priceless treasure of faith.

Finally, there was Saul (later known as Paul). We first hear of Saul as one who persecuted and abused Christians (7:58–8:3; 9:1–2). He perpetrated violence against Jewish Christians—his own people who had converted to Christianity. Saul believed he followed God in his efforts to stop the growth of this new movement called "the Way" (9:1–2). Saul experienced transformation through a direct encounter with a resurrected Jesus on the road to Damascus (9:3-19). In a dramatic interchange, Saul heard a voice from heaven exclaim: "Saul, Saul, why do you persecute me?" (9:4). Recognizing the voice as God's, Saul asked, "Who are you, Lord?" (9:5). The response Saul received to his query must have shocked and troubled him. The voice replied, "I am Jesus, whom you are persecuting" (9:5).

Saul returned with a repentant attitude to join the very people he was persecuting. He reflected a posture of repentance when he wrote, "I am the least of the apostles, unfit to be called an apostle, because I persecuted the church of God. But by the grace of God I am what I am, and his grace toward me has not been in vain" (1 Corinthians 15:9–10). With their experience of persecution so fresh, some in the early church had a difficult time believing Saul's transformation (Acts 9:20–31). Yet reconciliation occurred because the transformation in Paul's life was authentic. When God speaks into our lives, we need to remain persistent in our repentance until others can affirm the authenticity of our transformation. Reconciliation was possible in Antioch because Saul— renamed Paul—met a Jesus on the Damascus Road who invited him to let go of his trust in traditional religion and take a journey for God that would lead him to Caesar's palace in Rome.

Conclusion

Let us hear the call to partner with God at the forefront of reconciliation in the twenty-first century. We must become a first-century church in the twenty-first century. We embrace God's will by engaging in the ministry of reconciliation. We sustain reconciliation through creative partnerships, and we safeguard it through courageous and bold action. Finally, reconciliation becomes possible when we fully embrace and welcome the process of transformation that occurs when we choose everyday to follow a Jesus who is the same yesterday, today, and forever.

QUESTIONS FOR DISCUSSION

1. What inspires you most about the first-century church? Why?

2. Do you agree that the early church believed that reconciliation was God's will? Why or why not? Do you believe that reconciliation is God's will? Why or why not?

3. Describe some creative partnerships that you have observed or participated in. What were the key ingredients in these partnerships?

4. Why does reconciliation need to be safeguarded? What are some ways this can be accomplished?

5. What is the relationship between personal transformation and institutional transformation in the ministry of reconciliation? Can one occur without the other? Can one be sustained without the other?

NOTES

1. Richard J. Foster, *Streams of Living Water: Celebrating the Great Traditions of Christian Faith* (San Francisco: HarperSanFrancisco, 1998), 119.

2. Cheryl J. Sanders, *Saints in Exile: The Holiness-Pentecostal Experience in African American Religion* (Oxford: Oxford University Press, 1996), 32.

3. Sanders, *Saints in Exile,* 28; Foster, *Streams of Living Water,* 114; and Vinson Synan, *The Holiness-Pentecostal Tradition: Charismatic Movements in the Twentieth Century* (Grand Rapids: Eerdmans, 1971, 1997), 93.

4. Foster, *Streams of Living Water,* 113.

5. Ibid., 123.

6. Sanders, *Saints in Exile,* 30.

7. See Curtiss Paul DeYoung, *Coming Together: The Bible's Message in an Age of Diversity* (Valley Forge, Pa.: Judson, 1995), 13.

8. Foster, *Streams of Living Water,* 124.

9. Samuel G. Hines, *Experience the Power* (Anderson, Ind.: Warner, 1993, 1995), 92.

10. For a discussion on the traditions about Peter's martyrdom, see Michael Grant, *Saint Peter: A Biography* (New York: Scribner, 1994), 152–54.

11. Craig S. Keener, *The IVP Bible Background Commentary: New Testament* (Downers Grove, Ill.: InterVarsity Press, 1993), 357.

12. Ibid., 357–58.

5

The Church as a Reconciling Fellowship

Living Together as Witnesses to God's Agenda[1]

SAMUEL GEORGE HINES

EVERY WEEK IN CONGREGATIONS ACROSS THIS PLANET OUR HURTS AND our hopes bring us together to seek ways we may be equipped for maximum effectiveness in our topsy-turvy world. As God's church, we are called upon to witness in a world that is plagued by alienation, isolation, nationalism, racism, and other grave injustices that mislead us in our evaluations of one another. Religious idealism frequently takes us on utopian trips under the hallucinating influence of unrealistic possibilities. This results in a short-circuiting of our declared objectives to find the healing and biblical resolutions necessary in conflict situations. The Bible exhorts us, among other things, to be sober and watchful as we face the realities around us. We need to ask probing questions as we search for significant and realistic answers. We need then to be diligent in following up these processes by intentional and expeditious actions. As Christians we must enter into binding covenants with one another, which will underwrite our godly lifestyle and demonstrate the practical implementation of our fellowship in Christ. We cannot close our hearts to the instruction of the Holy Spirit who emboldens, sanctifies, and sensitizes us to become responsible and faithful stewards of the message and ministry of reconciliation.

As a God-ordained reconciled community, the church must develop, facilitate, and nurture these covenants of reconciling relationships between all people everywhere and at all levels of society. The church does not exist in a vacuum. Injustice and evil are all around us, but we cannot allow ourselves to become overwhelmed by the problems. We serve a God who has a record of being able to handle situations that seem impossible to human beings. As people of God, we cannot sit around griping about the rise of immorality and violence in homes, cities, and across the globe. We are not at liberty to be mere observers of the dismantling of family life, the disaster of public education, the increasing environmental pollution or the debacle of urbanization. Jesus expects the people in his church to be caring and commonsense stewards. He once told his disciples a parable about a king and his servants. Before going on a long journey, the king gave some of his servants specific assignments with the command, "Occupy till I come" (Luke 19:13, KJV). The inherent message was that, until Jesus returns to earth at the end of the age, the people of God are agents and heralds of all God's truth, including the message of holistic reconciliation between God and humankind and between hostile people. We are God's ambassadors entrusted with the word of reconciliation.

The Paralysis of Sin

The church needs to remain alert and aware that the world around us is a sinful, secular, materialistic society. This is not an indictment. It is a confession that every human being must make. We must heed Paul's words, "Be careful then how you live, not as unwise people but as wise, making the most of the time, because the days are evil. So do not be foolish, but understand what the will of the Lord is" (Ephesians 5:15–17). This means that we must not, like ostriches, bury our heads in the sand to avoid trouble. We must keep looking all around us and always be ready and willing to become part of the solution to the problems that plague our world. Sin, disobedience to and defiance of God, has created problems for all of us—vertical problems with God and horizontal problems with the people around us. The Almighty is treated as a stranger in the very world he created for community. The result is that humanity is trapped in alienation, hatred, stereotypic separations, and all kinds of other disconnections. Separation from God causes us to live in brokenness as though the main link in a chain is missing.

Traditional sociological perspectives, misguided loyalties, and unnatural biases box us in culturally, economically, nationally, philosophically, racially, and religiously. But for the Christian, the texture of the material that makes the box in which we hide is not the issue. The color or thickness of the rope that ties down the lid of the box is irrelevant. When you are boxed in, you are boxed in! The members of our various fellowships come, emotionally and spiritually confined in these boxes, to the churches of their choice. They come from the secular city to meet within our sacred walls and hear about the Holy City. What they hear must connect their agenda with the divine agenda. They must be encouraged to embrace the liberating message of reconciliation between God and human beings and the glorious possibility of reconciliation between all persons who have been estranged from one another, for any reason. Jesus expects the local church to include teaching on reconciliation and how to keep the peace as part of the discipling ministry. As Jesus told his disciples in the Sermon on the Mount, "Blessed are the peacemakers, for they will be called children of God" (Matthew 5:9).

Breakdown of Communication

The breakdown in our ability to communicate with one another in the human family is another sign of sin. The very words that we use cause problems—black and white, haves and have-nots, majority and minority, rich and poor, conservative and liberal, sacred and secular, right and left. All of these words have meanings attached to them that make it difficult to talk to one another without offending or misunderstanding one another. In spite of our global network of high-tech communication, we are still strangers to one another. Words that should be used purely descriptively are used destructively. The result is that persons who are disconnected from one another spiritually and often socially and economically throw words like stones at one another from their distant points of estrangement. The hearers then interpret the words through their stereotypic lenses.

This breakdown in communication creates situations in which we not only put labels on other people, but we also pass judgment, estimate worth, and attach value to other human beings on the strength of our biased understanding of these terms. We use words to add or subtract meaning and significance from the intrinsic human dignity and worth of individuals or groups. This aspect of the problem is very clearly observable in children. Up until their adolescent years, they will play, work, and learn together with very little, if any, friction regarding race, color, class, or religious beliefs. As they grow older, they learn about prejudicial attitudes and discriminatory actions, either by observation or direct instruction from the adults around them. They then copy, internalize, and begin to act out the feelings and behaviors that result from the socialization to which they have been exposed.

The people in our congregations hear and read these pejorative terms. They also see all kinds of culturally and racially slanted presentations in the media. They remember them and have them in their hearts as they sit in our pews and bow at our altars. Church leaders must take responsibility to create opportunities for mutual sensitization, face-to-face dialogue, and the building of meaningful relationships between people of both sexes, all ages, classes, nationalities, and differing persuasions. The local congregation must exist as a reconciling fellowship.

Disillusionment in Change

Like death and taxes, change is an inevitable feature in our society. In spite of the best efforts of those who attempt to preserve the status quo, this world constantly changes. Only a reckless person stands in the way and attempts to block all change. We call a person irresponsible or mischievous who roams around a marketplace changing labels and price tags, saying that this will create change. By the same token, this sort of superficial action, in the context of human interactions, is not a source of healthy, peaceful, or lasting change within or among human beings.

Significant changes are taking place in our value system, some for better and some for worse. We live in a whirlpool of changing forms, ideas, and structures. Some people welcome these changes while others feel threatened or frightened by what they consider the causes of the troubles of the times. Still others dismiss the changes they observe as trivial and superficial. Their passion is for more radical change, which may or may not be justified. The cry for change is louder in some places than in others, but it is almost always there.

In order to realize their dreams, hopes, and plans, some advocates of economic, educational, and social changes in a nation see bloody revolution as the only means for effecting the necessary political change in a given country. Up to the present time, the revolutions in various nations have not created the utopias promised or anticipated. Those who use the ways of the world to transform the world become slaves to politics, as well as to various ideologies and systems, while vainly crediting themselves with revolutionizing the world. In our day, superficial modifications, expensively achieved at the cost of thousands of human lives and the destruction of physical means of survival, are being hailed as liberating revolutions. Almost without exception these cataclysms have proven not only ineffective in creating beneficial changes in society, but they have notoriously dehumanized persons and diminished human rights.

As we have often found to be true in the past, tinkering with systems of governance will not bring about real or lasting change in a home, community, or nation. This degree of change happens only when the focus of the hearts of the people involved is changed from blame and hate to reconciliation. In every nation, laws need to be reviewed and revised, when necessary, in order to ensure justice for all people in the land. But changing the laws will not bring an end to unjust practices or abusive and violent actions by persons who have irrational and ungodly motivations for their behavior. A large number of the advocates of reconciling changes in the world take the route of tinkering with the social, educational, and political machinery but do not go on to help people to see their need for change in internal attitudes about God and other people. Our churches have a God-given responsibility to help guide people to follow the route of holistic reconciliation built on love for, faith in, and submission to God and love for all people around them.

Materialism and the Misuse of Facts

Enslavement to the mastery of things (materialism) and the misuse of facts are other aspects of the effect of sin on our human natures. No matter which area of the world one may live in or visit, the East, the West or the Third World, the prevailing ethos of materialism is the same. People at every level of society seem consumed by the desire to possess, distribute, or produce things, as well as to control other persons. This leads to a deadening of concern for the welfare of others and the development of disputes and even wars between family and community members and among nations.

Facts offer the final evidence in the world's reckoning of any matter, but the easiest way to confuse people is by misusing facts. People who do not recognize the supremacy of God will rearrange facts to gain their own ends. In some circles these misapplied facts are strangely equated with truth. Material things and misinterpreted facts are deified in our age, and people worship at their shrines. For example, nuclear armament is a fact, not a truth. However, the best that we seem able or willing to do about it is to enter into compromises and unstable treaties. The nations of the world have not shown the authority, creativity, or wisdom to deal decisively with the truth of the immorality of the whole issue. The truth is that the purpose of personal and material resources in the world is for the enrichment of life, not for its annihilation. To present the fact of the possession or threat of the use of nuclear arms as a means of maintaining peace in the world misrepresents a fact as the truth.

In the absence of spiritual wisdom and power, the world resorts to economic, political, and technological power to stabilize society and establish peace in our time. With the mastery of material and scientific things, we have become increasingly selfish and greedy. The majority of us invariably use what we have to get more, even if, in so doing, the dignity of others is violated or their lives are destroyed. We have allowed the control of facts to deny us the freedom only truth can bring. The end result of all this is phenomenal inequity and escalating moral decadence. For any or all these reasons, we stand apart from one another in terror, because we perceive other human beings as enemies to be feared, hated, and ultimately defeated. Vast numbers of the people in our churches are held captive by materialism and commercialism. They have been brainwashed by misspoken or misperceived facts. We all need to hear, learn, and internalize God's truth if we ever hope to emerge from our boxes and view the world and other people from God's vantage point.

In Jesus, the Son of God who took on human flesh, a new being was revealed on planet earth as a prototype of the merging of the divine will with that of human beings. It is as we receive Jesus to be lord of our lives that the "lenses" in the eyes of our inner beings are corrected to 20/20 vision, spiritually. We become changed, new kinds of persons on the inside, who are able to discern truth and gain a new view—God's view—of God's self and of the circumstances and people around us.

The Church and the World

I must now move on to deal with the convictions that people in local congregations bring to their interactions with the world. To be precise, I should probably substitute "ought to bring" for "bring" in the preceding sentence. The most eloquent rhetoric that deals descriptively with the problem can do very little more than amplify the groaning of the oppressed, the growling of the oppressors, and the sighing of those who lie in between the two groups. Some persons in each of these groups are sensitized and motivated to see righteousness and justice prevail, but by their own confession they feel helpless. It is necessary for us, the people of God, to take time to identify the bleeding wounds of emotionally bludgeoned individuals and broken communities. With the enabling of the Holy Spirit, we have to develop the compassion that will allow us to recognize the internal lacerations of those who have been made to endure the dehumanizing pressures to which the powerless are subjected by the powerful. These findings must trigger the enlightened interpretation and compassionate response of the people of God to the misuse and abuse of power.

The Church as God's Living Witnesses

Before Jesus ascended into heaven, he told his disciples, "But you will receive power when the Holy Spirit has come upon you; and you will be my witnesses in Jerusalem, in all Judea and Samaria, and to the ends of the earth" (Acts 1:8). This was a mandate, not only to his followers at that time, but to all those who would come after. Throughout the ages the church has had the mandate to bear witness to all the truth of God. We are to lead the world in acknowledgment of the supremacy of God and the oneness of all humanity. Each individual bears within himself or herself the stamp of the image of God, so we are all image-bearers of the Almighty. Our primary conviction must be that the God of unlimited power, unerring justice, and unfailing love has "made of one blood all nations...to dwell on all the face of the earth" (Acts 17:26, KJV). We embrace God's point of view as the perspective from which to observe and judge the facts and events of our lives here on this planet. God is the Lord over things as they are as well as over things as they ought to be. As creatures of God's hand and instruments of the divine purpose, our concerns must transcend our own interests and reach over to fulfill "the good pleasure of his will" (Ephesians 1:5).

The local church is not just another community organization or social institution. God intends local congregations to be reconciling communities created in Christ and brought to the acknowledgment that "all this is from God, who reconciled us to himself through Christ, and has given us the ministry of reconciliation" (2 Corinthians 5:18). In affirming the church's God-consciousness, the apostle Paul articulated for an imperfect congregation at Corinth their responsibility. This responsibility is based on the great commandment that Jesus himself affirmed: " 'You shall love the Lord your God with all your heart, and with all your soul, and with all your mind.' . . . 'You shall love your neighbor as yourself' " (Matthew 22:37,39). Love for God and our neighbor is the primary calling of human beings. The opposite of love is estrangement, alienation, separation, and disconnection, which are some of the consequences of sin that entered the world by the disobedience of our first parents.

God did not accept the disruption of sin as the ultimate state for the human race. God acted in justice to punish sin and in love to redeem the sinner by sending Jesus to earth to become the perfect appeasement for our sin. God took the initiative to accomplish reconciliation, executing and administering a perfect plan with benefits and responsibilities for all persons who believe. The people of God's church are therefore directed to declare and demonstrate the same love that God exhibited in sending Jesus. The apostle Paul directs us to develop the same mind that was in Christ Jesus (Philippians 2:5–11). Each community of believers must be noticeably bonded together in covenants of faith and love that create unmistakably christocentric fellowship. This is a supernatural oneness that can only be accomplished by God.

We as the church of the New Testament, like the nation of Israel in the Old Testament, have been given the opportunity, backed by God's promises, to break out of the boxes in which we are trapped. Our leader, Jesus, "made captivity itself a captive" and "gave gifts to his people" (Ephesians 4:8). The Hebrews, as you recall, were slaves in Egypt. They were considered to be a motley crowd in an insignificant subculture. Then God effected their deliverance in answer to their cry and welded them together into a liberated community with a sense of direction. They were then free to pursue their destiny. Whenever they disobeyed or forgot their covenant with God, they defeated their own purpose. God promised to make them a great nation and promised that through them all the nations on this earth would be blessed (Genesis 12:2–3). The omnipotent God came through on both counts. The church, made up of people who believe in and make an intentional decision to do God's will, can always bear witness to the miraculous truth that God, through Jesus, delivered us from sin and broke down the walls of division between all persons.

It is important to underline here that the "liberated" can box themselves in if they have the wrong perception of freedom. The local church is commissioned to share the news of the liberating gospel and the inexhaustible love of God with all people. They become partners with God, fellow-laborers with one another, and "ambassadors for Christ" (2 Corinthians 5:20). We are not to be just a huddle of saints focused on maintaining ourselves and the domain within our sacred walls. We are called to become authentic witnesses and significant representatives of our Lord Jesus Christ. The church sees Jesus as the pioneer and perfecter of divine possibilities for all people. The local congregation must always seek to declare and live out the two major possibilities of life, which are to love God totally and love our neighbor with the same passion that we love ourselves. We must prepare the way for others to experience this miraculous, redeeming love by proclaiming our confidence that love works and by being consistent in providing the evidence.

The Holistic Appeal of the Gospel

The people of God, individually and as a group, must be totally convinced of the oneness of all life. We are whole persons and live and move as whole beings. The church must not accept the artificial dichotomies created by the world to keep people apart, nor absorb the beliefs and false assumptions on which these are based and fed. Whether a person is oppressed by guilt of personal sin or by unemployment, underemployment, or unemployability—that person is oppressed. We may succumb to death as victims of physical illnesses caused by viruses or other bacteria, organ dysfunction, or social diseases. We may be hurt because of the physical assault of a personal enemy or the injustice of the nation in which we reside. All of these happenings cause anguish and sorrow. Since a large proportion of these result from sin, they must be addressed, not only physically, but also spiritually, prophetically, and redemptively. Local churches must accept the assignment to preach the whole gospel to the whole person—body, soul, and spirit. We must be persuaded that it is urgently necessary to determine how the sin of the soul and the sin of the system (bodily or politically) can be targeted and beneficially affected by the gospel.

So long as we are in the midst of an unbelieving society in which righteousness is so rarely lived out, justice will be denied and love will be perverted. The church community must herald the truth of the kingdom of God, calling attention to the godly resources for restoration and renewal that the world in general so blatantly disregards. We must remember that we are not called upon to either build or bring in the kingdom. We are to bear witness to its reality! We must be aware that we cannot live on Mount Olivet, where the question was asked, "Lord, is this the time when you will restore the kingdom to Israel?" (Acts 1:6). We have to live in the world and mingle with all kinds of people. Thankfully, we live on this side of Pentecost, appreciating and appropriating the response that Jesus gave to the question. He stated that there is knowledge about the future of the kingdom that is not presently available to the church, but that our empowerment for witnessing would come when we allowed the Holy Spirit to occupy and fill our beings with God's power. Disciples of Jesus Christ cannot embrace nationalism or any belief that will hinder them from spreading the truths of the gospel.

Many persons become totally mired in designing political solutions and traditional religious jargon to find solutions to the problems that are almost engulfing us. In actual fact, the problems are not overwhelming. Whether the troubles are in homes, cities, rural areas, high or low echelons of society or among nations, we become overwhelmed by them because we depend on our own strength and knowledge rather than seeking the wisdom of the all-wise, all-powerful God. The church must make it clear that Jesus does not restore things to what they used to be or commit to bending history in order to pacify the insistent demands of our finite minds. Jesus, by the work of his Holy Spirit, moves us on to where we ought to be in his judgment. Individuals reluctant to give up old comforts for new realities interrupt the onward mobility plan God has for their lives. As God directs us, we must relinquish old forecasts and move into arenas of new fulfillment. God's word for us is not "again" but "anew." Christians, the people of God through faith in Jesus Christ, are offered enabling power for kingdom living here and now. This is not a utopian dream of total freedom from all trial and trouble, but of righteousness, peace, and joy in the Holy Spirit. Communities of believers that experience and advocate these three graces will model and mediate the reconciliation that God initiated.

The Church's Commission

Jesus did not address his Great Commission to denominational bureaucracies (for there were none), but to believing individuals in local communities. Jesus said to that group of eleven disciples, "Go therefore and make disciples of all nations, baptizing them in the name of the Father and of the Son and of the Holy Spirit, and teaching them to obey everything that I have commanded you. And remember, I am with you always, to the end of the age" (Matthew 28:19–20). The strategy for carrying out this commission is not based on an imperative that demands that we go out teaching or preaching. In the everyday course of life where traffic with the world is not only inevitable, but desirable, Jesus admonished us to disciple, not just to make converts.

One sermon or conversation with an individual may produce a convert, but discipling that person takes time and personal commitment. We have to build relationships with those being discipled. Here, interaction is more vital than articulation. Actions mean more than words. This is a key factor in the ministry of reconciliation. *We cannot just tell people about reconciliation and walk away from them!* We have to spend quality time with persons who have been in situations of alienation. We have to help them understand that through the reconciling work that Jesus did on Calvary, we and they can be reconciled to God and receive the grace and love we need to repent and forgive in order to be reconciled to estranged persons around us. We have to help them understand how to take action to right wrongs they have committed, as well as maintain peaceful relationships with those to whom they have become reconciled.

The person being discipled needs to be tied in with the body of Christ—a local church. By helping new Christians in their study of the Word and encouraging them to allow the Word to abide in them, we can monitor their spiritual maturity. Biblical illiteracy accounts for much of the inaccuracy with which we interpret and apply the Scriptures to our own lives. This is patently true when we attempt to proclaim and practice reconciliation. The Bible teaches that horizontal reconciliation goes far beyond academic exercises and goes much deeper than economic, educational, political, or social initiatives. All of these play a part, but the defining factor is the change of heart brought about by vertical reconciliation with God. The church has to be delivered from the superficiality of simplistic solutions, continuous dialogue that does not lead to decisive action, and from the temptation to apply ineffective social and other bandages where drastic spiritual surgery is needed. Continual and consistent efforts must be made to help people grasp the true meaning of God's Word for their lives that they will "not be overcome by evil, but overcome evil with good" (Romans 12:21). This means that when people wrong us, our response as Christians is to recognize the evil but not allow either that person or his or her actions to determine our agenda. Our response, based on Jesus' example, is to find some way to mount a campaign of good in behalf of the person or persons who have hurt us. With the coming of Jesus into this world, we have learned that we must always resist evil. We cannot and must not be lured into returning evil for evil.

Reconciliation is not a human-sized job. It is a God-sized undertaking. Jesus has accomplished the work of making the way clear for the possibility of reconciliation between God and human beings and between people who are enemies. The church now has to help people understand how to turn enemies into friends. We have to accept the blessing ourselves and proclaim it to others so that they also can receive. With the guidance and empowerment of the Holy Spirit, we can move the mountains of distrust, discrimination, greed, immorality, prejudice, racism, ungodliness, and violence. None of this will happen unless we are willing to lay our lives on the line for the cause of reconciliation. We have to show ourselves ready and willing to cross the bridges that we build across all chasms of alienation wherever they may exist. The local congregation, at its best, is a community that demonstrates what life is like when God's kingdom comes and his will is done on earth as it is in heaven. The standard of ethics for the church, local and universal, must be kept at the level where it does not reflect conformity to the world, but transformation by the renewal of the Spirit of God. Individual believers, local fellowships, and the universal church of God must be quintessential examples of God's reconciling grace.

QUESTIONS FOR DISCUSSION

1. Describe the ideal local church. Have you ever experienced this? In part? For a brief moment? If so, how were you impacted?

2. Describe a reconciling fellowship. In your opinion, can a local congregation be a reconciling fellowship? Why or why not? Can a denomination be a reconciling fellowship? Why or why not?

3. Why is communication so important in the creation of a reconciled community?

4. Cite some examples of the effects of materialism and the misuse of facts in our society. In what ways does this affect the local church and its witness to God's reconciliation?

5. Samuel Hines states, "Reconciliation is not a human-sized job. It is a God-sized undertaking." What do you think he means by that statement?

NOTE

1. The body of this chapter was originally presented as a message preached by Dr. Samuel Hines at the historic South Africa Christian Leadership Assembly (SACLA). That watershed convocation was held in Pretoria, South Africa, in 1979. It is estimated that approximately 5,000 civic and church leaders were in attendance. This first, nationally advertised, cross-cultural, cross-racial gathering had been banned by the then ruling government. It proved to be one of the first times in South Africa's history that people from all the separate groups living in the country met publicly under the same roof. This message has been referenced as being the defining word for that convocation. It blazed a trail for the convening of several Renewal and National Initiative on Reconciliation conferences.

   Dr. Hines visited South Africa at least yearly for ten years and used that time to minister, behind the scenes and away from the media, to individuals and groups from all the varying races, at all levels of the society. He, with his covenant brother, John Staggers, brought people together for mutual sharing and airing of their grievances and led many to effective and long-lasting reconciliation. Many of these persons went on to lead the country in the dismantling of apartheid.

6

A Case Study in Reconciliation

Implementing a Ministry of Reconciliation in a Local Congregation

SAMUEL GEORGE HINES

I HAVE LIVED IN WASHINGTON, D.C., FOR TWENTY-FIVE YEARS. WHEN I ARRIVED in Washington, I realized that I faced a challenge, a privilege, a responsibility, and a threat. All of these were wrapped up together in my assignment as the second pastor of the congregation that I had been called to serve in the nation's capital. I succeeded the congregation's founder, who had led the congregation for fifty-seven years, so it took a few years for me to be accepted as their pastor. The church is eighty-four years old and has had only two pastors!

This small church in Washington, D.C., had succeeded in building *koinonia*—fellowship—among themselves. Most of the members had been together for a long time, and they looked out for one another. I discovered that the pastor and his wife, who had no children of their own, had literally housed more than 50 percent of that congregation at one time or another. Many had come from the South as young people to attend Howard University or to find jobs. Almost every member I visited had lived or had a relative who had lived in the pastor's house. These people did not call this man "elder" or "pastor," but "my dad." That was a wonderful community into which to enter, if you could get in—and I got in. The former pastor and his wife had no scandal attached to their lives; they were meticulously clean. He was dictatorial, but the people accepted him as a benevolent dictator. He was a pioneer. When he spoke the earth trembled and the church moved.

From Maintenance to Mission

I recognized that my predecessor was a pioneer and I was not. I could not duplicate his pioneer style of operation. I quickly observed that the church had grown up with a maintenance orientation—a ministry primarily, although not exclusively, focused internally on its own membership. I felt led by God, while consolidating their internal nature, to guide the congregation into becoming a mission-oriented church, involving ourselves in ministry to the neighboring community and then farther afield. That caused pain, because the change tore at people's inner sensitivities, pulled them out of security and comfort, and led them to put themselves at risk in a hostile society from which they had taken refuge for years. I took people who had effectively answered the call to come out of the world and sent them back into that world as witnesses and ambassadors. How do you do that? I decided to get to know and love the people, and therefore busied myself visiting them in their homes, walking around the community, and ministering in the parish. In the Lord's work here on earth, it is never a matter of either/or between maintenance and outreach. The intentional emphasis must always remain both/and, as we lead people into understanding and practice of the ministry of the kingdom of God.

An Intentional Teaching Ministry

Another thing I did was to guide this congregation into redefining their understanding of the word and concept of *"church."* I had to do this with their input. This was not easy. I initiated a course for all the members. In the first class session, I asked them to write down whatever came to their minds when I said the word church. The responses to that stimulus were most fascinating. They convinced me that I needed to engage in a long-term, intensive teaching ministry. I settled on the expository style of preaching as the most effective tool for teaching Christian discipleship and mission, and I began preaching from the epistle to the Ephesians on Sunday mornings. I continued for over a year in that glorious epistle, where Paul defines the church, clarifies ministry, and outlines the divine agenda as God's plan to bring all things in heaven and earth and under the earth together in Christ Jesus (Ephesians 1:10; 2:14).

We had numerous retreats, which allowed people to participate, respond, and share in a relaxed atmosphere. As I continued to preach, we held more retreats, workshops, seminars, and conferences. People in the congregation were encouraged to visit new places and become exposed to people whom they had never met. Some of these were people whom they had classified as being evil. We had a great time breaking down walls and coming to love God and one another. The parishioners and I established dialogue and a common understanding regarding the biblical concept of "church." We also prayed and prayed some more! We had early morning prayer meetings, midday prayer meetings, and midnight prayer meetings. Some people thought we overprayed! As we studied God's Word, loved one another, and prayed, minds began to open and sensitivities awakened. We became aware of new aspects of ministry.

A vision emerged as a result of these retreats. We developed a goal statement that we often repeat together that reminds us of the biblical mandate under which we must operate in the Washington scene and the world context in which we find ourselves. It says:

> We are ambassadors for Christ in the nation's capital, committed to be a totally open, evangelistic, metropolitan, caring fellowship of believers. To this end we are being discipled in a community of Christian faith, centered in the love of Jesus Christ and administered by the Holy Spirit. We are covenanted to honor God, obey His Word, celebrate His grace, and demonstrate a lifestyle of servanthood. Accordingly, we seek to proclaim and offer to the world a full cycle ministry of reconciliation and wholeness.

Proactive Reconciliation

Because I was a new pastor in a new place, I thought it advisable to meet with (among other people) the leaders in the metropolitan area. One of these was the Honorable Walter Washington, who was then the mayor of Washington, D.C. After introducing myself as a new pastor in the area, I assured the mayor that I needed his help and asked if there was anything I could do to help him in the city. The mayor welcomed me, and we had a good dialogue. Two days later the mayor called to ask me to see him. When I went back downtown, he said that he wanted to make me a commissioner in the city. I was very surprised and asked him to give me a chance to pray and think about it. I went home and thought about it and talked and prayed with my wife, who is my lifetime partner, and two other people. I came to the conclusion that one of the worst things I could do was accept an office in the city at this time!

I returned to the mayor's office and told him that I could not accept his offer for several reasons. First, I was too new to the city. I could not be a commissioner in a strange city. I needed to know the city first before I could fill such an office. Second, I did not yet know the people in my congregation whom I was leading as pastor. I did not want to take positions out in the community that could not be backed up by relationships at my home base. Third, I had researched the manual on commissioners and discovered that they had to be the mayor's supporters, and he must be able to count on them at all times. I had to be freer than that. I wanted to be able to applaud him when he did right and speak out boldly when he did wrong. Since I did not think that commissioners had that kind of freedom, I could not accept such an appointment. So I went back to my church and into the community to learn and serve in freedom. The mayor said that one thing I could do to help him would be to keep the church open on Sunday evenings, and I have done that throughout the years of my pastoral ministry.

Several things emerged from my encounter with the mayor. First, I became part of an interdenominational group of ministers who formed a coalition to help redeem and restore young people in the city. Our churches opened several foster homes, and we rescued many young persons from all kinds of evil. Also, at this time in Washington, many people hated the police and called them "pigs." Our church organized a monthly meeting between the police and the community residents. Both groups would meet and talk about problems and possible solutions, which was a big step in those days, and the results were quite beneficial. For the first time we had a police officer on foot patrol in our community, and that helped to put our community back in shape. The people and the police began to work together. Third, when we noticed that seniors in our community had nowhere to go for socializing and recreation, we started something called Senior Neighbors and Companions Club (SNACC). Out of that we had some senior citizen marriages and other interesting developments. One fellow went back into business after being retired for many years. Camaraderie flowed between the people, and much talent was brought into action again.

In the meantime I met a Christian activist who became my covenant brother. If you do not have a covenant brother or covenant sister, you need one (in addition to your spouse if you are married). We were bonded together. We pledged in the name of Christ that we would support one another till death parted us and that we would lay our lives down for each other. We would consider nothing impossible to accomplish in the city if we knew it to be God's will. We would work together at all times. We began to meet every Monday for Bible study and prayer in my home. I continued the intensive preaching and teaching ministry, and the church continued in prayer. At the same time, I met for prayer once weekly, very early on Wednesday mornings, with a small group of Christian leaders, governmental officials from the city, and some members of the church fellowship. We consistently and passionately sought God's mind for the divine will concerning the texture and scope of our ministry in the city.

Urban Ministry Emerges

Then God sent a young woman from California to enlarge our ministry in the city. She came to our church unexpectedly and said, "God told me to come here and give my life to ministry in Washington. Can you help me?" She agreed to meet with us every Monday morning thereafter. With my wife and covenant brother, we spent about three hours on Mondays together praying, reading God's Word, and talking about God's will for the city of Washington, D.C. As a result, God brought into being a coalition called Washington Urban Ministries. By this time, the young woman, who was Caucasian, had become a member of a very prestigious Presbyterian church in Washington, D.C. She began to expose us to that church and the new minister who had just arrived from California. We began making friends with him and his wife.

The plan was for my covenant brother, the new pastor, and I to become real brothers. That proved to be difficult initially since men often do not open up to one another easily. We tend to guard our "turf" very jealously, because many of us consider that a part of our male strength. At least that is the facade we put up to project an image that we are strong and independent. One day my covenant brother and I shared with this Presbyterian pastor that we felt God urging us to invite him to partner with us in inner-city ministry. He assured us that he loved us and frankly admitted that he faced many challenges in his new church and could not put the inner city on his agenda at that time. We accepted his response and assured him of our prayers. Both that pastor and I continued to preach and teach about the meaning of mission in our separate churches.

In the meantime, our two churches began doing things together, such as work days, potluck meals in one another's homes, Bible studies, and sensitivity sessions. My wife and I often taught classes at that church. One day we three men met in the community around my church for a work day. Once again my covenant brother and I told the Presbyterian pastor that we had been praying about him being our covenant brother, and with his wife praising the Lord beside us, he said, "I yield, brothers. What do you want me to do?" We told him that we did not want him to do anything but be our brother, and we would learn to love one another and work together. So we began praying, reading God's Word, meeting in each of our homes, and having retreats together. We prayed and sought God's mind for ministry in our city. During one of these times, we came to the certainty of our status as covenant brothers and that we would lay down our lives for one another. This personal covenant with one another led to the godly partnership between this Caucasian Presbyterian Church and our predominantly African American Holiness Church.

The following steps emerged as our churches moved into the reconciling process:

1. God empowered one or more laypersons with a vision for unity in each of the churches.

2. Church leaders and some members from each congregation committed themselves to the study of God's Word and unceasing prayer.

3. The pastors met together, at a sacrifice of time, to get to know and bond with one another.

4. Lay coordinators who had reconciliation on their minds were found in each church (this was not an easy task). They did not have to know all about it but had to be willing to learn. The two individuals began to meet together to pray, study God's Word, and socialize. (They discovered that they had the same wedding anniversary date, so they and their spouses started to celebrate their anniversary together.) This highlights a very important principle in bringing about reconciliation between individuals and groups. Until and unless people get to know each other on a face-to-face basis, to resonate with the joys and sorrows, the successes and failures that each experiences, to learn to value each other for their intrinsic worth as persons, and to let go of stereotypic thinking, there will never be genuine, lasting reconciliation between them.

5. The lay coordinators developed reconciliation committees in each church. They began to discover what the needs were and where

suitable resources were located. Their job was to tell us their findings and how we could get things together to do practical ministries in the city.

6. The main church body in each fellowship was kept informed of all developments, and many people from both churches became involved. There was not an avalanche of volunteers, but enough to get the work done.

7. We had to do a lot of sensitivity exercises and a lot of learning about the theology of reconciliation. We had to learn to *do* our theology instead of just *talk* about it. We had to learn to survive racism in both our congregations and our church communions. We had to learn to fight social taboos on both sides of the fence. We never had a single quarrel about doctrine, because our discussions centered around ministry. We talked about our mutual needs in each fellowship and how to get God's work done.

The Enduring Story

One of the most heartening signs in America today is the resurgence of interest in and commitment to reconciliation. During the 1960s when the Lord quickened within me a preoccupation for the reconciling ministry, very little current literature, sacred or secular, had been written on the subject. The civil rights agenda which was originally based on the nonviolent teachings of Jesus Christ (as well as the modeling in the life of Mahatma Gandi of India), was sacrificially lived out by the late Dr. Martin Luther King, Jr. That agenda has, for the most part, moved into the adoption of a sociopolitical vocabulary and focus. In a nation trapped in secular concepts, biblical language is not seen as being relevant or acceptable by a large section of the population. Today, however, we hear "reconciliation" on the lips of many, from householder to governmental leader, from laborer to child advocate, from entertainer to judicial arbitrator, from heads of state to virtually every religious group. All proclaim the necessity for reconciliation. The lasting fellowship and ministries between our two congregations in Washington, D.C., is a beacon to the strong possibility of reconciliation between people of different races, cultures, and beliefs.

The relationship remains very strong. That pastor and his wife eventually retired and left the city. When a new pastor came to the Presbyterian church, he and I bonded together and moved forward. There is no easy one- or two-step method to accomplish reconciliation in any area—certainly not in the domain of interracial, intercultural, and interdenominational relationships. Because "with God nothing is impossible," reconciliation is always possible when all sides work at it. We know that we still have a long way to go in proclaiming, teaching, modeling, and intentionally practicing reconciliation, but we will not give up. We are not always on the mountain top, but our two congregations continue to network with an increasing number of others to keep the message alive and the flame alight. We are ambassadors for Christ in the nation's capital. We continue to be an evangelistic, metropolitan fellowship of believers and to plumb new levels in our partnership with God every day.

QUESTIONS FOR DISCUSSION

1. What is the difference between a maintenance-oriented church and a mission-oriented church? List the attributes of each. Which style of ministry is better suited for reconciliation?

2. How does teaching about biblical reconciliation prepare a congregation or individual for the practice of reconciliation?

3. What kind of programs or projects can help facilitate reconciliation? Recall some that you have observed or participated in. What made these programs or projects effective?

4. What does it mean, in practical terms, to develop a partnership with another person? Or for two congregations to partner? What are the key points in the steps that these two congregations took?

5. How does the idea of a covenant brother or covenant sister enhance the concept of partnership?

SECTION 3

Practicing the Ministry of Reconciliation

The Truth about Forgiveness

An Essential Component in the Practice of Reconciliation

SAMUEL GEORGE HINES

THE WILLINGNESS AND ABILITY TO FORGIVE CONSTITUTE TWO OF THE most crucial aspects in the process of reconciliation. Our reluctance to forgive those who have abused, hurt, or offended us until or unless they come to us in repentance blocks this process toward unity. Reconciliation always involves a continuing cycle of repentance and forgiveness. Unfortunately, many of us withhold forgiveness, even when we can see the signs of repentance from the offending person(s). The people of God must lead the way in demonstrating an attitude of proactive forgiveness, which we learn from the study of God's Word and from Jesus' lifestyle. Forgiveness is the primary truth of God's salvation for the human race and a prominent part of the uniqueness of our Judeo-Christian heritage. If we extract forgiveness from the content of our belief, the entire body of our faith collapses and we have nothing to sustain our witness to the grace and mercy of God. The lack of personal experience in receiving God's forgiveness deprives us of the assurance of the affirmation of Jesus, "Your sins are forgiven" (Luke 7:48). Until these words become truth to us, we are bound by the devil, condemned to spiritual darkness, and hopeless about eternal life with God. Forgiveness is a basic and essential component in the process of reconciliation. None of us can understand or extend forgiveness to others if we do not first get an inside look at and appropriate the forgiveness of God.

In the book of Numbers we find a powerful passage about God's forgiveness. Moses interceded in prayer by expressing his zealous concern for the preservation of God's reputation. He feared that the outpouring of God's wrath upon the rebellious Israelites would tarnish the glory of God that had been established by gracious and supernatural dealings with them on their journey from Egypt. In the following passage, Moses prayed to God:

> "And now, therefore, let the power of the LORD be great in the way that you promised when you spoke, saying,
>
>> 'The LORD is slow to anger,
>> and abounding in steadfast love,
>> forgiving iniquity and transgression,
>> but by no means clearing the guilty,
>> visiting the iniquity of the parents
>> upon the children
>> to the third and fourth generation.'
>
> Forgive the iniquity of this people according to the greatness of your steadfast love, just as you have pardoned this people, from Egypt even until now."
>
> Then the LORD said, "I do forgive, just as you have asked . . . "
>
> *(Numbers 14:17–20).*

This passage illustrates that forgiveness is neither a public relations strategy nor a sales pitch that God adopts occasionally to maintain a good name. Inherent in the divine nature, forgiveness is God's way of delivering human beings from the weight and condemnation of sin. God personalizes a forgiveness plan for lifting and carrying far away the burden of our iniquity and the record of our transgressions. From Genesis to Revelation, the authors of Scripture define God in infinite progression. All the facets of God's character reveal themselves in shining glory. Some refer to this as the overwhelming *Isness* of God, who is the great "I AM WHO I AM" (Exodus 3:14). The passage from Numbers offers us some definitive insight into the quality and substance of God's forgiveness.

Longsuffering—A Companion Virtue of Forgiveness

Moses quoted an earlier proclamation by God in Exodus 34:6 when he stated that "the LORD is slow to anger" (Numbers 14:18). I prefer the King James Version's translation, "The LORD is longsuffering." God suffers long and waits patiently for us, because that is the divine nature. God constantly reminded the Israelites then and reminds us now of the reason we escape immediate punishment. God is not blind to our disobedience and sin, slow and lacking in urgency, nor impotent and unable to act. God exhibits longsuffering as a companion virtue of forgiveness. Neither a forgiving God nor forgiven and forgiving people are ever eager for vengeance. When we practice endurance and are always ready to forgive, we don't experience a rush to release anger.

Rather than a one-time deal, forgiveness is a repetitive grace. In Matthew 18, Peter asked Jesus how often he would be required to forgive a brother who sinned against him. "Peter came and said to him, 'Lord, if another member of the church sins against me, how often should I forgive? As many as seven times?' Jesus said to him, 'Not seven times, but, I tell you, seventy-seven times'" (Matthew 18:21–22).

Peter gave what would have been considered a generous figure of seven times for making this allowance. Jesus responded clearly and unmistakably when he told Peter that no limit for forgiveness existed, as illustrated by the figure of seventy-seven times (many translate this seventy times seven). Jesus demonstrated the limitless extent of forgiveness in his first words from the cross when he said of his enemies, "Father, forgive them; for they do not know what they are doing" (Luke 23:34). As the people of God, one of the signs of our identity with God through Christ is our unity with one another. Unity will not be maintained for long among us unless we seek and practice the gift of longsuffering and the grace of forgiveness. Our God is a God of great mercy and kindness, always disposed to grant us forgiveness and pardon beyond our earning or deserving. Jesus once told his disciples, "Be perfect, therefore, as your heavenly Father is perfect" (Matthew 5:48).

Why God Forgives

What God does is based on who God is. Theology, the study and analysis of God's attributes and relations to the universe, begins and ends with the simple yet profound truth that *God is!* A great deal lies in between the beginning and the end, but the self-existent and unchanging God consistently and intentionally remains true to the divine nature. Inadequate understanding of God's nature leads to erroneous judgment of God's actions. Faith rooted in falsehood leads to deception. A lack of clarity about God's image leads to confusion about our own and everyone else's identity. Forgiveness is an attribute of the character of God and therefore must be true to everything that is true about God's nature.

The book of Numbers brings us to an outstanding level of reality in contemplating the structure of forgiveness:

- Forgiveness does not mean denial of guilt.

- Forgiveness is not a declaration of innocence.

- Forgiveness, from God's perspective, does not mean acquittal, because acquittal means that one is not guilty or that guilt was not proven beyond reasonable doubt. That angle does not arise with the all-knowing God. In God's reckoning, every human being is a sinner, and each sinner is guilty as charged. "If we say that we have no sin, we deceive ourselves, and the truth is not in us. . . . If we say that we have not sinned, we make [God] a liar, and his word is not in us (1 John 1:8,10).

Forgiveness does not change the facts; it transcends them. We must not bend forgiveness out of shape in order to make it fit some fantasy that we concoct in our minds. Forgiveness is the granting of pardon for sins committed. The verdict of a righteous God stands, but our relationship with this God changes through the act of forgiveness. God's forgiveness lifts the burden of the ultimate result of sin—separation from God.

Furthermore, the text in Numbers declares the tough truth that forgiveness from God does not necessarily break the connection between cause and effect. The word used in the original language of the Old Testament for "visiting" (Numbers 14:18) is often translated "'punishing." God is too wise and loves us too much not to leave in place the law of consequence, by which we are reminded that the way of the transgressor is hard and "the wages of sin is death" (Romans 6:23). Punishment removes the glitter and glamour from sinful actions. God does for us much more than we deserve by restoring our broken relationship and holding on to us with a love that will not let us go. In the same way, the church must be so in tune with God's Spirit that we learn, in increasing measure, how to love and forgive unconditionally, so that our broken horizontal relationships may be restored and we can remain at peace with the people around us. God often allows the natural law of cause and effect to operate within and around us as evidences of justice and as a call to moral responsibility.

Long before humanity knew anything about genetics, Moses recognized that the actions of one generation could affect future generations. Visitations connected with the normal results of sinful actions remind us of the right way and the wrong way to conduct our living. Each choice we make has consequences. Forgiveness is not the mushy behavior of an indulgent God or of weak people. Forgiveness provides strong and radical deliverance from final spiritual and often physical destruction and removes the fearful expectation of God's judgment. Forgiven and forgiving people live truly liberated lives empowered by God's love.

This brings us to the point of repentance or contrition. Repentance, like a magnet, attracts and pulls on God's forgiveness. A magnet cannot draw objects that do not exist. The ever-present nature of God's forgiveness impels us to repent and assures us that we will receive mercy. A repentant attitude propels the people of God in reconciling processes. Repentance is always necessary to engage in the process of reconciliation. As Christians, our readiness to forgive those who have wronged us must be so evident that we attract their repentance. Jesus once told his disciples, "For I tell you, unless your righteousness exceeds that of the scribes and Pharisees, you will never enter the kingdom of heaven" (Matthew 5:20). We should always maintain contrite hearts toward God, because contrition unlocks the door to an otherwise rebellious, murmuring heart and brings us the blessing of forgiveness from God. "If we confess our sins, he who is faithful and just will forgive us our sins and cleanse us from all unrighteousness" (1 John 1:9).

Unforgiven people with unforgiving spirits weigh down any congregation and impede God's mission in the world. They sit like tons of lead on the wealth of God's riches and blessings for the church. Every unpardoned sin of members of a fellowship puts the brakes on the church's mobility and delays the arrival of the revival for which the church prays and waits. We are becoming a global society full of revenge and bitterness. Let us remember that forgiveness is most often extended when asked for in contrition and repentance. Whether we get mad or try to get even, an unforgiving or unrepentant spirit is at work. Jesus taught us to pray, "And forgive us our debts, as we also have forgiven our debtors." He also said, "For if you forgive others their trespasses, your heavenly Father will also forgive you; but if you do not forgive others, neither will your Father forgive your trespasses" (Matthew 6:12,14–15).

Moses, the patriarch and prophet, learned the value of intercessory prayer early in the course of his traveling with the people of God. In this section of the journey through the wilderness, Moses prayed, "Forgive the iniquity of this people according to the greatness of your steadfast love" (Numbers 14:19). He recognized that in calling upon God for deliverance from divine wrath, the measure of forgiveness that anyone seeks from God is determined by the character of God and by the Almighty's record established from the beginning of time.

The Strength of Forgiveness

God's forgiveness upholds us when we experience the weight of guilt and anchors us when the stormy seas of life rock our boats. Even if God chastens and corrects us through divine discipline, the assurance of forgiveness can and will give us courage and strength to keep holding on. None of us will ever experience true peace without God's forgiveness. Sometimes we go a little distance in life on the strength of our own temperament, virtue, or skill, but very soon we learn that we need God's forgiveness to enable us to get through each day. When life presses us down or tears us up, God's forgiveness can lift us up and make us whole again.

When we experience forgiveness and become forgiving persons, we enjoy many unique blessings. Forgiveness from God clears the way for a holy righteousness to direct our lives. Forgiveness clears our vision so that we can see life with clarity and focus on the things that please God. We also discover relief from the burden of harboring grudges and plotting endlessly for revenge. Forgiveness unblocks the emotional, mental, and spiritual channels of our lives so that God's grace and love can flow through us. (We must remember that God's forgiveness may leave natural laws in place.)

We need to revisit the language of forgiveness and restore the symbols of forgiveness in our homes and in God's church. Intentional acts of forgiveness must be initiated if they are not being practiced. In communities and nations throughout the world, policies facilitating and promoting forgiveness and rehabilitation of wrongdoers need to be put in place and consistently maintained. Multiplying the number of prison facilities has not reduced the crime rate. Forgiveness is God's way of dealing with the iniquity and perversity of the human race. Forgiveness must become a central core of our dealings with each other if we sincerely desire to live in a world where peace and reconciliation become the order of the day.

QUESTIONS FOR DISCUSSION

1. Why is forgiveness an essential component in reconciliation?

2. Why does Hines call longsuffering a companion virtue to forgiveness?

3. Why does God forgive? What does it mean to be forgiven by God? What does it not mean?

4. How does an unforgiving attitude affect individuals, their families, their churches, and their communities?

5. What does the experience of being forgiven by God do for us? Can you witness to the power of God's forgiveness in your own life?

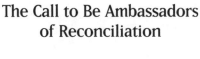

The Gospel Ministry

The Call to Be Ambassadors
of Reconciliation

SAMUEL GEORGE HINES

THE CHRISTIAN ASSIGNMENT—WHAT I CALL THE GOSPEL MINISTRY—IS biblically clear. The apostle Paul offered a wonderful summary of this gospel ministry when he wrote:

> Therefore, knowing the fear of the Lord, we try to persuade others; but we ourselves are well known to God, and I hope that we are also well known to your consciences. . . . For the love of Christ urges us on, because we are convinced that one has died for all; therefore all have died. And he died for all, so that those who live might live no longer for themselves, but for him who died and was raised for them.
>   . . . So if anyone is in Christ, there is a new creation: everything old has passed away; see, everything has become new! All this is from God, who reconciled us to himself through Christ, and has given us the ministry of reconciliation; that is, in Christ God was reconciling the world to himself, not counting their trespasses against them, and entrusting the message of reconciliation to us. So we are ambassadors for Christ, since God is making his appeal through us; we entreat you on behalf of Christ, be reconciled to God. For our sake he made him to be sin who knew no sin, so that in him we might become the righteousness of God (2 Corinthians 5:11,14–15,17–21).

Paul's manifesto informs us that we are the community of God's new people who form a new delegation in the world carrying out the divine engagement of restoration, renewal, and reconciliation. Any confusion about our assignment comes from our own making. Neither God nor the Bible contributes to the ambivalence that many of us experience as we approach our task. We must reaffirm our commission, refine our roles, and renew our commitment to serve as assigned in this divine enterprise. God has a one-item agenda listed in one expressive and inclusive word: *reconciliation*. Even with many variations of strategy and a great variety of related activity, the agenda remains the same. In a universe that has been plunged into chaos by the catastrophe of sin, we must work ceaselessly toward restoring and reconciling all people unto God. We must not allow any obstacles—resistance, weariness of the flesh, bombardment of the mind, or fatigue of spirit—to diminish our zeal as we pursue the gospel ministry. Paul's words to the Corinthians reveal to us the compelling motivation for pursuing the ministry and proclaiming the message of reconciliation.

The Compelling Motivation for Reconciliation

The passage in 2 Corinthians 5 deals, first, with the compelling motivation for reconciliation. The apostle Paul clearly gives the triple stimuli that should prompt and urge us to aggressively persuade men and women, boys and girls to be reconciled to God. The first stimulus for our motivation listed in this passage is something about which we do not often consider—*"the fear of the Lord"* (5:11). The King James Version calls it the "terror of the Lord." Paul could not allow divisive forces to separate him from the saints at Corinth because of his fear of the Lord. He could not stand by while suspicions, assumptions, traditions, gross misunderstandings, and prejudices disrupted the peace and dismantled the unity he worked so hard to establish at Corinth. The care with which he confronted the troublemakers and the troubled is partly his response to what he identified as the "fear of the Lord." This fear of the Lord is a sobering awareness of God's holiness, an awesome recognition of God's justice, and a nudging remembrance that our motives and our deeds are always under divine scrutiny. We will all appear before the judgment seat of God's Son to give an account of our behavior. Princes and peasants, the prosperous and the poor, the powerful and the powerless, the haves and the have-nots will all have to give an account at the judgment and should therefore scrupulously seek to please God.

Our society has seen a great diminishing of this fear of the Lord. We witness the consequences of the absence of that fear in the unparalleled corruption, violence, and viciousness in evidence in our world. When people lack or lose the fear of the Lord, despicable forces corrupt their passions, enslave their wills, inflame their emotions, and drive them to a reckless abandonment to evil. Godly fear instructs our ethics, manages our morals, corrects our conduct, and restores our broken relationships. Godly fear calls for justice, regulates righteousness, and urges mercy. The fear of God also promotes holiness and insists on purity of heart while it holds us together in peace. God-fearing people are bold people. Those who fear God have nothing else to fear! We are learning that it is unsafe to live in a society that has lost its fear of the Lord.[1]

The second stimulus for our motivation is *constraining love*. Paul wrote, "The love of Christ constraineth us" (2 Corinthians 5:14, KJV). Paul feared the Lord on the throne, and he loved the Christ on the cross. The reconciler encounters an irresistible force in the love of Christ—the same love that caused Jesus to embrace the cross also motivates his followers. The love of Christ constrains us to bear up under suffering and to exercise our best judgment in deliberately renouncing all self-indulgence, while directing us to live in conformity to him who died for us all. Just as Jesus Christ set his heart on humanity while yet in a state of moral deformity and spiritual delinquency, so we must exclude no one as we reach out to bring in *all* for whom he died and rose again.

More than a fleeting emotion, Christ's love is an energy and power that locks us in and holds us together with all kinds of people. Love always elevates our commitment beyond the level of those whom we serve, to reach him in whose name and for whose sake we render the service. It is not just our love *for* Christ, it is the love *of* Christ in us, that shapes, molds, and intensifies our dedication to the task of restoring to spiritually dead people the life they have lost and their purpose for living.

This mysterious love merges the visible and the invisible and breaks down the barriers that serve as walls of separation behind which we so often hide from one another. When the work of God is done only out of the fear of the Lord and is not permeated with Christ's love, the work becomes difficult and joyless. People who come to God only out of awe and never feel the pull of Christ's love may yield to his authority without ever surrendering joyfully to the embrace of his overwhelming love. Unfortunately, in the world in which you and I live, very little is really done based on love. It is sadly true that unloved children often become love-starved adults who in turn bear their own unloved children brought up in an unloving environment. We have an obligation as Christians to break this cycle of apathy and antipathy so that all may flow together in love and peace. We must accept nothing else.

In Christ we have more than a model of service based on love. He is the living fulfillment of a promise he made when he said: "And I, when I am lifted up from the earth, will draw all people to myself" (John 12:32). The apostle Paul said in 2 Corinthians that the crucified Christ supplied more than a magnet to draw people upward. He also provides the glue that holds us together with purpose and passion. The meaning of the word "constrains" derives from two Greek words—*sum* and *ecco*—meaning, "I hold together." It is the same love, shed abroad in our hearts by the Holy Spirit, that motivates us to be persistent in persuading others to accept the responsibility to reconcile with others. As Christians we have the opportunity and obligation to fight against our own prejudices, the divisive cultures in which we are born and reared, economic pressures, political systems, and whatever else may divide us from one another. We have the obligation to resist all these destructive forces in the conquering name of Jesus. We must, like Paul, make a decision not to allow our own hurts and disappointments to plunge us into ambivalence, double-mindedness, or lukewarmness in our support of the divine agenda. Christ within us enables us to stick with our difficult assignment.

The third stimulus for our motivation comes from what the apostle Paul called the *power of a new creation*. Paul wrote, "So if anyone is in Christ, there is a new creation: everything old has passed away; see, everything has become new!" (2 Corinthians 5:17). The apostle Paul knew how easily we become totally enslaved to old ways of thinking. Myths and traditions become patterns in our processes of thought and judgment over time. On the other hand, the apostle Paul had a transforming experience. He had personal experience to support his claim that whole patterns can be changed, so that we see beyond the popular labels that we give one another—labels of race, nationality, class, economics, culture, religion, and a thousand other categories we use to stereotype and manipulate one another. Paul knew that this could change because he had been changed. A true Christian knows that God can bring about this change of perspective and perception described by Paul because it has happened to him or to her. The apostle Paul, exercising an elevated intelligence, carefully gives credit to God. He says that we cannot achieve this on our own, because it is all God's doing. We must do what God created us to do in Christ Jesus. Our function must be controlled by divine design and not by human desires.

The Ministry of Reconciliation

Once motivated, we must acknowledge that the ministry of reconciliation is hard work. Reconciliation is not a bright idea concocted by some sociologist or philosopher. Reconciliation is God's all-inclusive plan, open to everyone, which deals adequately with every obstacle and every hindrance that sin puts in our hearts and in our way. This plan confronts every objection and every objector, submitting the problem to the death and resurrection of Jesus Christ. When motivated people change through the work of God within them, they then become vocal and visible agents of reconciliation. How does this change come about? What does it mean? When people yield to the lordship of Jesus Christ and the refining power of the Holy Spirit, they experience a change. In the words of the Amplified Bible, they are: "No longer fashioned after and adapted to the external, superficial customs of this age, but transformed or changed by the renewal of their minds . . ." (Romans 12:2). They demonstrate what they proclaim when they call people out of their boxes to reconciling actions and ministries. Gospel ministry occurs when the reconciled become servants, with and for others, to produce additional evidence of the effectiveness of what God has done in Jesus Christ. One of the drawbacks of this vocation to which I belong is that we are given different titles: "clergyman," "reverend," "pastor," and sometimes "minister of the gospel." "Minister of the gospel" is not a professional title belonging only to a few theologically trained people wearing robes and turned-back collars. The passage in 2 Corinthians 5 erases that idea completely. Rather, the title applies to all of us who have been reconciled to God and must now become reconcilers.

The ministry of reconciliation is a costly enterprise. Reconcilers do not sit in ivory towers talking about reconciliation. Jesus said that they deny themselves, take up their crosses, and follow him. Reconcilers do not necessarily see what is going to happen, but they work hard to make the right and godly thing happen. We urgently need workers in reconciling ministries. Are you one of God's reconcilers? Are you privately or publicly, personally or corporately, in high places or low places, on a main stage or backstage working to help others to be reconciled to God and therefore to be reconciled to one another? Godly reconciliation cost Jesus Christ his life, and Paul was not about to take this ministry lightly.

The Reconciling Message

Motivation! Ministry! Message! Paul says that there is a word to be spoken, a message to be proclaimed, a logos to be heralded. Reconciliation is a powerful, loving, creative word that needs to be uttered in the midst of all the discordant noises of human strife and hatred around us. Maybe you would declare that you are ignorant about that matter and no one should look to you, or maybe you do not care enough to become involved. You may say that that is someone else's job, not yours. Maybe you are arrogant enough to say that if everyone would just leave you alone, you could work out the situation yourself. Some may even say that they have tried everything but have found no solutions. The apostle Paul would not identify with any of these attitudes.

The message of 2 Corinthians 5 is very clear and very intentional when it says that God has taken the initiative (v. 18). God has come in Christ to do an on-site job of reconciliation. God's purpose is not to charge our sins to our account, but to purge the record. To that end, Jesus Christ, the sinless one, took upon himself the sin of the whole world so that he could be free to bestow his righteousness upon us. That is the message! God has done it! No one has to go through life torn up on the inside because of estrangement from God. All of us, everywhere, can find the peace of God in Christ. In every situation in which we find ourselves, we ought to be clearly pleading and persuasively beseeching others to listen to the message of reconciliation.

During an airplane flight, I asked a man, "What is the message of your life?" He said, "What is the question?" I repeated the question, but he could not give me an answer. Once I threw that question out to some people who were being interviewed for a position in a church publishing house. The question "What is the message of your life?" threw them into complete confusion. I asked that same question of persons who expressed a desire to serve on the mission field. They usually responded as if I had asked them to explain the atom bomb. Do we know the message of our life? What are we on this earth to say, and where are we to say it? Each of us always conveys a message. Our choices, words, actions, values, ethics, morals, appearances, and lifestyles, as well as the way we manage our relationships, invest our resources, and arrange our priorities all convey a message. Where we go and what we do when we get there, the company we seek, the influence we wield, the service we render, the stand we take or don't take, the sacrifices we make—these, too, convey a message. Paul wrote that our message is, "Be reconciled to God" (2 Corinthians 5:20).

Conclusion

You cannot set the world right if you yourself are not right with God. Make sure that your motivations are right. Become personally involved in some aspect of the reconciling ministry. Get the message out wherever you go. Do not sit idly by and let alienation from God and polarization between people disfigure and dismantle this beautiful world that God has made. Diversity is God's idea. Divisiveness is of the devil. The gospel ministry is our enterprise, which is to win back a lost world of men and women, boys and girls to the Lord. If we choose to be on God's side, we can make a difference. May God make us different and use us to make a difference in the world.

QUESTIONS FOR DISCUSSION

1. What compels and motivates you to be interested or active in the work of reconciliation? Relate some events or experiences that were turning points for you.

2. What is compelling and motivating about the fear of the Lord, love, the power of a new creation?

3. Why is it important to have personally experienced reconciliation? Why is personal testimony powerful?

4. Define "the ministry of reconciliation." Who can serve in this ministry?

5. What is the message of your life?

NOTE

1. Here are a few additional Scriptures that can help us when we fight the battle against the satanic influences in our society:

"The fear of the LORD is the beginning of wisdom" (Psalm 111:10).

"Fear God, and keep his commandments; for that is the whole duty of everyone" (Ecclesiastes 12:13).

"Do not fear those who kill the body but cannot kill the soul; rather fear him who can destroy both soul and body in hell" (Matthew 10:28).

"His mercy is for those who fear him from generation to generation" (Luke 1:50).

"If you invoke as Father the one who judges all people impartially according to their deeds, live in reverent fear during the time of your exile" (1 Peter 1:17).

"Honor everyone. Love the family of believers. Fear God. Honor the emperor" (1 Peter 2:17).

8

A Healing Word for a Hurting World

Preaching and Teaching the Message of Reconciliation in Today's World

CURTISS PAUL DEYOUNG

NOTED PREACHER JAMES FORBES TELLS OF AN EXPERIENCE THAT HAPPENED to him in 1974 at the World Conference on the Holy Spirit. The conference was held in Jerusalem that year, and he was assigned to preach a sermon prior to a healing service that featured well-known faith healer Kathryn Kuhlman. Forbes finished his sermon quickly since most of those gathered anticipated the healing service. He preached from Mark 7:34, where Jesus said to the man whose ears were closed, "Ephphatha." (Mark translated this Aramaic word as "Be opened!") After Dr. Forbes finished his sermon, Kuhlman demonstrated the power of her healing ministry as two hundred individuals proclaimed healing.

Kathryn Kuhlman said to those at the service, "I'm not the healer. It is God who is doing the healing." James Forbes, commenting on his thoughts at the time, writes: "I was deeply moved by the power of her ministry. Actually, I was a bit jealous. I felt that being a professor and a preacher was insignificant compared with her extraordinary gifts." Then Kuhlman spoke directly to the pastors on the platform. She said, "Pastors, you can be healers too if you let the power of God work through you." Forbes thought to himself, "Um hum, sure."

At the end of the service, a woman and her husband came up to Rev. Forbes. The woman said to him, "The Lord led us to come and say something to you. My husband was here, hoping to be touched by Kathryn Kuhlman because he had a hearing problem. He was completely deaf in one ear." The woman continued, "My husband was waiting for Kathryn so he could be healed. He wanted you to hurry and get out of the way, so he could receive his healing. Then when you said that word, 'Ephphatha,' his ear was opened! The Lord wanted us to come and let you know that even through the preaching of the word, healing can take place."[1]

I believe that even through the preaching and teaching of the Word, reconciliation can begin to take place. Our hurting world certainly needs a healing word. This episode from James Forbes' ministry reminds us of the healing power of the Word. I believe that the power of the spoken Word offers a unique balm in the healing ministry of reconciliation. Professor Martin Brokenleg witnesses to this power when he writes that "for Lakota people, the spoken word has a power that the written word does not. If one is making an important point, as in promising to do something, it can be believed only when it is spoken. Moreover, what is stated in front of witnesses is considered a vow. . . . The preacher, then, has accomplished something important since thoughts and affections have been put into words."[2]

If what Martin Brokenleg says about the Lakota people also rings true for other people, to some degree, then teachers and preachers have a significant calling in this ministry of oneness with God and with others in the human family. They put into words the "thoughts and affections" of God. The preacher and teacher deliver the Word to the community of God so that each member might be equipped to activate his or her ministry of reconciliation.

The message of reconciliation is God's powerful healing word. Therefore, teachers and preachers speak for God as instruments of spiritual healing—an awesome and audacious task. James Earl Massey, in his book *The Burdensome Joy of Preaching,* speaks of "the burden" of this holy endeavor. He says that the "sense of being burdened as God's speaking servant is compounded by the attendant awareness of being personally exposed. One does feel exposed, for one is speaking not only *about* God but also *for* God."[3] This personal exposure as God's spokespersons reminds us that we must first experience and then continue to experience God's work of reconciliation in our own lives before sharing this news with others. It is a humbling gift that God uses those of us who teach and preach to inspire people to receive God's healing touch and equip them to reach out to others with reconciling love. As ambassadors of reconciliation, "we not only *present* a message, but also *represent* its Sender."[4]

In this chapter, we will look at the practice of preaching and teaching the biblical message of reconciliation. Insights will be drawn primarily from my study of preachers and the art of preaching, as well as from my own experience as a preacher of reconciliation. I have found in my own ministry that what I suggest in this chapter also directly applies to the teaching ministry of reconciliation.

Content—The Word Made Flesh

The most important aspect of teaching and preaching is the content of the presentation. In the opening chapters of the Gospel of John, the writer declares what should be the core content of reconciliation preaching and teaching. In John 1:14, he states the theme for his entire gospel, "The Word became flesh and lived among us. . . . " John directs his readers to the mystery of God taking on human flesh and living among us—God's on-site job of reconciliation. The Jesus event—birth, life, death, resurrection, and abiding presence—is at the center of any proclamation of reconciliation. John reminds us that the Word needs to take on flesh in order for us to comprehend the gospel's relevance for our life.

In the first two chapters of John's gospel, he establishes Jesus' divinity through John the Baptist's announcement, "Here is the Lamb of God who takes away the sin of the world!" (1:29) and his testimony: "I saw the Spirit descending from heaven like a dove, and it remained on him. I myself did not know him, but the one who sent me to baptize with water said to me, 'He on whom you see the Spirit descend and remain is the one who baptizes with the Holy Spirit.' And I myself have seen and have testified that this is the Son of God" (1:32–34). John's inclusion of the episode of Jesus' miracle of turning water into wine at Cana further confirms Jesus' divine status (2:1–11).

After John had demonstrated that Jesus was God in human flesh, he wanted the readers to fully comprehend the purpose of God's visitation. To understand the implications of the incarnation of God, the reader must appreciate the full story of Jesus Christ as it unfolded. In the third, fourth, and fifth chapters, John declares the relevance of the gospel story by weaving together Jesus' encounters with four individuals. John's gospel is not a chronological study of Jesus' ministry, but rather a theological exploration of the meaning of the incarnation of God. These four narratives, describing Jesus at work in the lives of people, inform us of God's intent. They demonstrate the fulfillment of God's one-item agenda. The four persons featured in the four episodes are: Nicodemus, a woman from Samaria, a royal official, and a man lying by a pool in Bethesda.

In John 3:1–21, we learn of a Pharisee named Nicodemus who quietly and secretly crept through the side streets of Jerusalem to make an unannounced, unanticipated, and unusual visit to Jesus. This theologian, known as "Israel's teacher," was Jesus' peer. In John 4:1–42, Jesus met a woman from Samaria at Jacob's well. As we noted in chapter 3, she was perceived by society as off limits to Jesus because she was a Samaritan, a woman, and considered an immoral woman besides. In John 4:46–54, Jesus met a royal official who asked Jesus to heal his son. This man's elite royal status gave him power over the Galilean teacher. The fourth individual, a paralyzed man in Bethesda (5:1–18), had laid for thirty-eight years beside a pool waiting for someone else to help him get his healing. He was probably an embarrassment to any "self-respecting" person in his society.

By reading through the first five chapters of the Gospel of John, we learn that when God came to earth in human form, his coming introduced an inclusive and reconciling love. Jesus found room for everyone in his ministry. Like John the gospel writer, our teaching and preaching must first begin with the Word made flesh—Jesus Christ. The content of our message of reconciliation needs to speak to individuals in our society from all cultural contexts, to both women and men, and to those marginalized by others and those isolated by their hunger for power and control. "Christian preaching" (and teaching), as theologian Eleazar S. Fernandez writes, "is the proclamation of God's liberating, saving, and reconciling love as witnessed in the life and ministry of Jesus and the 'Christic' community that revolved around him."[5]

Jesus Christ—the reconciler par excellence—inhabits the very center of reconciliation teaching and preaching. In the fall of 1997, Claudia May, a professor at the University of St. Thomas (St. Paul, Minnesota), and I worked together to create a course on reconciliation. We taught the class in a local congregation and then at the university. We pondered for some time and sought God's mind regarding an appropriate title. After prayer, God led us to "Jesus—The Way to Reconciliation." The core content of all reconciliation preaching and teaching must be Jesus Christ—the Word made flesh—the Way to reconciliation.

Interpretation—The Language of Experience

Unfortunately, we cannot just simply announce that Jesus is the way to reconciliation. Our own interpretative lenses shape the content of our preaching and teaching. The interpretation of those listening to our words affects the impact of our message. Theologian Jung Young Lee reminds us that teaching and preaching are "a form of giving recognizable shape to the divine presence." This requires us then to "take cultural and ethnic contexts seriously."[6] Interpretation takes form not only within our cultural and ethnic contexts, but also by our gender, race, economic status, social class, geographic location, and a host of other factors. The person who proclaims the message of reconciliation must intentionally embrace the challenge of a lifelong learning curve in order to understand a wide range of perspectives. We must become fluent in the language of experience, our own and that of others.

Preaching professor Lucy Atkinson Rose reminds us that our teaching and preaching can "reflect multiple life experiences by avoiding claims concerning what is human or universal and by cautious use of the pronoun 'we.' " She adds, "I remember how often I have listened to a preacher describing what 'we' do or feel or think, and I was aware that the statements might reflect the preacher's reality but they did not reflect mine; 'I' was not included in the preacher's 'we.' "[7] Rose's concern has merit given the multiplicity of worldviews operating in our day. Race, gender, class, nationality, or other identifiers cannot become the "we" of experience. The messenger of reconciliation must learn to navigate these various perspectives with the intent of sharing the good news of God's love. When we claim our family relationships as children of God, we discover our common ground—our shared humanity.

We can never fully know the experience of another person. Culture, gender, race, class, and other ways in which we designate our social location create an even greater distance in our ability to understand. Yet we should not be content with this reality. We can intentionally work at gaining a partial knowledge of the experience of others; partial is the best we can accomplish. (Even couples married for decades cannot read each other's mind.) An even more significant avenue open to us is to know God's thoughts better. Since God is our creator, God is the one being who completely understands each person. In fact, God understands us better than we can ever understand ourselves. We can begin to better communicate the word of reconciliation as we combine a serious effort to increase the number of lenses we wear for interpretation and as we seek help from the God who created all humanity.

Below, the insights of three preachers from three different cultural settings illustrate the importance of gaining knowledge about the experience of others. Culture significantly impacts how we should communicate the message of reconciliation to a particular audience. Our choice of scriptural texts, images, and concepts may communicate in different ways, given the setting.

All knowledge, like all material goods, belongs to the collective community. . . . Consequently, all information and thinking begins and ends with the assumption that we are a single unit when together and that we will end up together. . . . Naturally, appeals to individual belief or individual salvation have no attraction to Native listeners.[8]

—Martin Brokenleg

Korean preachers are fascinated by the work of the Holy Spirit because of their background in shamanism, which is also a religion of spirits.[9]

—Jung Young Lee

In a racist society, not only are we forced to define ourselves as a race, which we usually would not, but we are also made to feel as in-between people, as people who are neither fish nor fowl, as people who live in the space between "accepted" definitions. . . . [Latinos] focus on other in-between people in Scripture, such as the Galileans, the Samaritans, and the Gibeonites, and to seek to discover their role in the history of salvation and of the world. . . . This may be a correction to much biblical hermeneutics, which takes for granted a simple dichotomy between Jew and Gentile, and therefore misuses some of the nuances, for instance, of the Galilean or the Samaritan.[10]

—Justo Gonzalez

If we take note of the cultural parameters suggested by the three preachers, we understand the importance of shaping the message of reconciliation in such a way that it communicates in the particular setting. In a context like that described by Brokenleg, we could focus on the outcome of reconciliation as leading to a greater sense of being God's collective community. Following Lee's lead, it would seem obvious that the role of the Holy Spirit in reconciliation, such as at Pentecost (and throughout Acts), would communicate the message well where there is

a strong belief in spirits (shamanism). Justo Gonzalez points us to particular people groups in the Bible whose lived experience is similar to
that of many people today. An invitation to preach or teach where there
are people from each of these three cultural settings (or more) sitting in
the audience provides us with quite a challenge. This is the growing
reality of the twenty-first century. The audiences expecting to hear a
word from God when we get up to speak bring a multiplicity of perspectives and life situations that influence what they hear. While this
has always been true to some degree, the age we call the postmodern has
very few givens. We all must become adept at the work of cultural
hermeneutics (interpretation).[11]

Illustration—The Engagement of People's Stories

The story is told of an African American man who engaged in the demeaning act of begging to address his hunger, because racism had limited his
opportunity to be self-sufficient. He approached the front door of a South-
ern mansion and rang the doorbell. When the owner, a white man,
answered, the black man simply stated his need: "I'm hungry." The white
man responded by asking him to retreat to the rear entrance. Food was
prepared and brought out to the hungry man waiting at the back door.
Then the white man asked the African American man to join him in blessing the food. He said, "Now you repeat after me, 'Our Father. . . .' " The
black man said, "Your Father. . . . " The white man corrected him, "Our
Father. . . . " The black man once again said, "Your Father. . . . " So the
white man asked him why he would not repeat the prayer. The hungry
African American man replied, "Well, Boss, if I say, 'Our Father,' that
would make you and me brothers, and I'm 'fraid the Lord wouldn't like it,
you making your brother come to the back porch to get a piece of bread."[12]

The above story comes from the not too distant past of racial segregation in the United States. It powerfully demonstrates what racial reconciliation required in that setting. The story also provides a good
example of how we can illustrate our messages in ways that engage
people's attention and communicate the content (reconciliation) we
seek to make plain. Samuel Hines wrote that we "must find ways to
make the text come alive and be meaningful for people today—how to
transfer the message from camel riders to jetsetters?"[13] The above illustration does just that. It takes the first phrase from the Lord's Prayer,
"Our Father," which had serious implications for God's oneness when

prayed by Jews and Greeks, and transferred it across time as a radical critique of racial segregation in the United States. In the same way, we must empower the biblical concept of reconciliation to live and breathe in our time.

Our preaching and teaching should always have a narrative feel to it as we share the greatest story ever told—God's act of reconciliation. Jesus used a variety of stories, images, and symbols to communicate his message. He used aquatic and agricultural images when he was near the water or traveling through rural areas. His stories came from the lives of both women and men. He used historical and cultural references in his teaching, such as the Queen of Sheba and Nineveh. When Jesus spoke to the Samaritan woman at the well, his understanding of Samaritan religious beliefs allowed him to tap into her expectation that the Messiah would be one who revealed all things.[14]

As we saw in chapter 3, there are many ways in which Jesus' life illustrates the intent of God to reconcile the world. During the Christmas season we can tell the story of how Jesus' family was visited by poor shepherds from Palestine and rich Magi from Asia, and then sought safety in a welcoming community in Africa. Strong women (Mary and Elizabeth) and strong men (Joseph and Zechariah) played important roles in the story. When Luke wrote his account of Jesus—a working class Jew from Galilee oppressed as a subject of the Roman Empire ruled by Caesar Augustus—he sent it to a Roman named Theophilus. During the Lenten season we can declare that at the crucifixion Jesus found support from an African (Simon of Cyrene) and faith in a European (Roman centurion). On Easter Sunday we can exclaim that first women and then men witnessed the empty tomb and the appearance of a resurrected Jesus Christ. Throughout the year we can proclaim that Jesus challenged his followers to "go therefore and make disciples of all nations" (Matthew 28:19).

Many stories from the Bible lend themselves well for illustrating the choices and complexities involved when one embraces reconciliation. Theologian Justo Gonzalez illustrates this through his novel use of the example of Moses.

In Hebrews 11:24–25 we read: "By faith Moses, when he was grown up, refused to be called a son of Pharaoh's daughter, choosing rather to share ill-treatment with the people of God than to enjoy the fleeting pleasures of sin." In this case, we are told that Moses had a choice. He could be part of the power elite of Egypt, or he identifies with the people of God. Before he opts for the people of God, he is part of the elite. Thereafter, he is part of the oppressed. Thus, the question of power and powerlessness does not refer only to two different persons or two groups, but also to two options of a potentially powerful individual.[15]

A person's life choices impact her or his options. Preaching and teaching reconciliation require us to call people to choose God's agenda. Biblical stories enable us to issue the call in a compelling fashion.

The stories we choose must speak to the settings in which we preach and teach. Sometimes we utilize stories from our own lives for illustration. We must carefully select episodes that bring illumination to the text we have chosen. Our own life stories must not be presented in a way that brings undue attention to our own exploits. The purpose of an illustration is to bring clarity and appeal to the salvation story. We should make sure that we share appropriate personal stories. Also, we must not attempt to get our own needs for pastoral care met through preaching and teaching. With these few cautions noted, our personal stories can provide a powerful bonding with listeners. Illustrations from our own life demonstrate the power of God's reconciliation. Such anecdotes may also inform listeners that we are cotravelers with them on the journey to live according to God's one-item agenda.

Style—The Artistry of Transformation

The message of reconciliation finds its core content in Jesus Christ and communicates in such a way to engage our stories through a variety of interpretative lenses. Noted 1800s preacher Henry Ward Beecher suggested that the style of the messenger is similar to that of an artist. In the very first Lyman Beecher Lectures series in 1871, Henry Ward Beecher stated that the preacher (and I add teacher) "is an artist—not of forms and matter, but of the soul. Every sermon is like the stroke of Michael Angelo's chisel, and the hidden likeness emerges at every blow." He continued that the preacher "is an artist of living forms, of individual colours: an architect of a house not built with hands—Jesus Christ the foundation."[16] The artist of the soul knows that her or his style impacts the final form in which the message is delivered. The style used by the teacher or the preacher enhances the possibility that transformation will occur. A style that breathes life into content informed by multiple interpretations and illustrated with compelling stories is necessary for the preacher or teacher to invite today's listeners to consider making Jesus Christ the foundation of their lives.

The first thing the teacher or preacher must learn regarding style is to embrace the gifts God has given her or him. We must not try to be someone else. The eloquent stylist of the nineteenth century, Phillips Brooks, suggested in his Lyman Beecher Lectures that, "To be yourself, yet not to be haunted by an image of yourself to which you are continually trying to correspond, that is the secret of a style at once characteristic and free."[17] Effective communication requires that we embrace our own unique giftedness. Yet we should also develop our style in ways that include the richness of other traditions.

I grew up in a church setting where sermons were typically twenty minutes in length and people sat quietly as they listened to the message. As I noted in chapter 4, in my early twenties I moved to New York City and became involved in a congregation in Harlem. The worship style contrasted significantly from that of my background. When I preached to the members of this congregation, I found that I slowed down and paused occasionally to provide a moment for verbal responses to points I made in the message. I also developed an ability to improvise when the response of the congregants or the move of the Holy Spirit indicated I should go in a new direction. My style of preaching and teaching emerged as a cross-pollination of different traditions. A synthesis of various elements from diverse perspectives creates a hybrid style quite useful for the ambassador of reconciliation.

Preaching professor Evans E. Crawford captures the challenge of style when he writes: "African Americans, for example, may have to work on a delivery style that best suits their ability and aspirations, while a European American may wrestle with how to handle the cerebration of the head with the celebrative urges of the heart. An Asian American may work on how to blend the contemplative with the celebrative."[18] The preacher and teacher of reconciliation attempts to bridge these traditions and preferences by exhibiting a style that is both authentic to herself or himself and appreciates diversity. Martin Luther King, Jr. was a wonderful example of this hybrid preaching approach. He merged phrases and poetry drawn from European sources with the folk idioms and method of delivery common among many African American preachers.[19]

Some things are essential to the style used by the messenger of reconciliation, such as using inclusive language and terms that engender respect. What feels natural for the teacher or preacher will determine some aspects of one's style, such as whether to use a manuscript or outline or to speak without the help of such aids. Other characteristics may relate to the particular cultural setting. Two examples follow. Teresa Fry Brown writes from an African American perspective:

> Failure to use a text as the basis of one's sermon is not preaching. At its best it is storytelling, and at its worst it is a travesty. African American theology of proclamation states that the word preached is not that of the preacher but that of God, who speaks through the preacher. Through the preached word, the justice, mercy, and grace of God are revealed in the congregation of the believers.[20]

Martin Brokenleg provides a Native American perspective:

> In Lakota oratorical tradition, it is considered bad manners to explain the message. Once a story is told, it is left to the listener to interpret and apply the message. Consequently, the groundwork must be laid carefully before the story is told. If a story is told well, then it will speak to the heart, not to the mind only, but to the whole person. That is, it will be understood at a deep and wordless level. Almost never will there be any discussion or compliment to a well-composed homily. The sign the message has reached the heart is signaled by eyes moist with tears and nothing more.[21]

Brown and Brokenleg identify important cultural aspects of preaching and teaching style. Given that transformation is a goal of reconciliation teaching and preaching, knowledge of proclamation etiquette in different cultural settings is essential. When delivering a message to multicultural audiences, respect for such nuances invites listeners into the salvation narrative.

Sermon Case Study

In December 1997 I stood before the congregation at the historic Bethel African Methodist Episcopal Church in Baltimore, Maryland. Frank Madison Reid III, one of the nation's most powerful preachers and the pastor of this twelve-thousand-member congregation, had invited me to preach. My challenge was to preach a sermon that took my passion for reconciliation and made it relevant to this congregation in Baltimore. I needed to combine content, interpretation, illustration, and style in such a way that it communicated to the people assembled on that Sunday morning. I chose Hebrews 13:8—"Jesus Christ is the same yesterday and today and forever"—as my text. My sermon title reflected the Christmas season, "Which Jesus Is the Reason for the Season?"

I anchored the content of the message with an overview of "yesterday's Jesus"—the Jesus of the Gospels. Then I moved from yesterday's Jesus to today's Jesus. At this point I began to utilize various interpretative lenses and brief illustrative images that called forth the liberation tradition of this historic African Methodist Episcopal congregation. I proclaimed:

> Today's Jesus never contradicts yesterday's Jesus because Jesus Christ is the same yesterday, today, and forever. We can check today's claims about Jesus Christ against yesterday's Jesus in the Bible.
>
> When the slave traders sailed ships named Jesus Saves and slave masters declared that their white Jesus endorsed the idea of blacks being slaves, people of African descent wearing chains, and some justice-minded whites, looked to the Jesus of the Bible and discovered that the Jesus of the slave trader and the Jesus of the slave master was not the same Jesus who was in the Bible.
>
> When Adolph Hitler seduced the Christian Church in Germany to embrace a Nazi interpretation of Jesus, Dietrich Bonhoeffer and a few others looked to the Jesus in the Bible and discovered that the Jesus of the Nazis was not the Jesus in the Bible.
>
> When White supremacists in the United States and in South Africa claimed to be following Jesus, Martin Luther King, Desmond Tutu, and a whole host of others looked to the Jesus of the Bible and discovered that the Jesus of white supremacy was not the Jesus in the Bible.

Given that this sermon was being preached the Sunday before Christmas, I next used interpretative lenses and brief illustrative images to focus on the text's relevance regarding the practice of Christmas and the challenges of materialism in our own age. I continued:

> At Christmastime, when we see a white baby Jesus lying in a sanitized manger and perfumed stable where materialism is the "reason for the season," we need to look to the Jesus in the Bible.
>
> When Jesus is presented as presiding over the perks and privileges of the "old boys" club in corporate board rooms, we need to look into the Bible and discover which Jesus we are following.
>
> We do not need a Ph.D. in theology to see that a lot of folks are creating images of Jesus Christ that serve their own agenda. But today's Jesus never contradicts yesterday's Jesus.

After lifting up liberation history and noting the materialism of Christmas, I then brought the message to the context of the city of Baltimore and to the lives of individuals hearing the message that morning. I said:

> Today's Jesus is also found hanging out in the same kind of places as yesterday's Jesus. The book *The Corner* tells the story of the drug culture operating at the street corners in many neighborhoods in the city of Baltimore. There's a woman in the book, Ella Thompson, who works at a community center with the purpose of inspiring "hope in the margins."[22]
>
> *The Corner* reminds us of where Jesus would be found. Jesus would be offering hope at the corner. There are far too many corners in our cities where the drug trade and the sex industry have the upper hand. Some of us may be called to join Jesus ministering at these corners.
>
> There are some other corners. There is the racism corner, the sexism corner, and the classism corner. Some of us need to be with Jesus at these corners looking for ways to provide the ministry of reconciliation. There is the materialism corner. There are people who are finding that material things are the way, the truth, and the life. And then there's the relationship corner. There are people who are investing all of their life in a relationship with a human being rather than in a relationship with God Almighty.
>
> Jesus is at those corners today, like he was yesterday, and we need to join him there. Because Jesus Christ is the same yesterday, today, and forever, we know that Jesus never contradicts himself, and we can find him hanging out in the same places as he was yesterday.[23]

While the written word cannot completely capture one's style, I preached in a way that embraced my own gifts yet honored the tradition of the congregation. I ended my message by celebrating the "foreverness" of Jesus Christ.

Person—The Practice of Our Proclamation

Henry Ward Beecher spoke a word in his day that remains true for us today: "A part of your preparation for the Christian ministry consists in such a ripening of your disposition that you yourselves shall be exemplars of what you preach."[24] The late Kelly Miller Smith, in his Lyman Beecher Lectures in 1983, described the importance of social crisis preaching. Yet he noted that "no matter how endowed the preacher is

with natural gifts, knowledge, and skill, the proclamation will be ane-
mic and ultimately ineffectual when the preacher is simply delivering a
message. Something of one's commitment expresses itself in the force
and power of the social crisis sermon."[25] James Earl Massey described
the late Howard Thurman, an exemplar of what it means to be a messenger of reconciliation, "as one who was under the management of his
message; he preached as an obedient servant of the truth which had
mastered him."[26] The apostle Paul testified that when Jesus appeared to
him, he said, "I have appeared to you to appoint you as a servant and as
a witness of what you have seen of me and what I will show you" (Acts
26:16, NIV).

We must practice what we preach and teach. The most powerful message we will ever preach or teach is the life we live. Our passion for reconciliation and our willingness to let it permeate our total being must
be more evident than our eloquence of speech. Who we are as persons
matters more than our public persona as teachers and preachers. To be
powerful preachers and teachers of the message of reconciliation, we
must place our total dependence on God. When we surrender our will
to God, something happens in our teaching and preaching. We experience what some call "being in the zone" and what others call the
"anointing." Massey describes this process:

> Anointed preaching therefore carries the hearer beyond the limited ben-
> efits of the preacher's personality and rhetorical abilities. Anointing from
> God makes the preacher an agent of grace. . . . and to allow the beyond-
> ness of God to break through with immediacy and authority in his
> words. . . . It is an awareness of being before God, challenged, called to
> account, claimed. It is a sense of Kairos, a special moment that is unique
> and individual.[27]

Conclusion

Samuel Hines in many ways exhibited what this chapter attempts to
communicate. He was one of the great expository preachers of the
twentieth century[28] and was also a powerful teacher of the Word. You
could depend on locating Jesus Christ at the core of any message by
Sam Hines. He also understood the various social locations from which
people interpret life and faith. He was comfortable proclaiming the

message of reconciliation in widely diverse settings. Hines was a master storyteller and used illustration effectively. His style remained consistent with his own gifts. Yet he could adapt to preach a two-hour sermon in a church where people had walked miles for a word from the Lord or a ten-minute message to individuals gathered to eat breakfast after spending the night on the streets and in shelters. He consistently walked his talk.

Samuel Hines modeled well what it meant to preach a healing word to a hurting world. He preached with a powerful anointing that could change the course of history. At Samuel Hines' funeral in January 1995, South African pastor Ross Main related the power of Hines' preaching in South Africa: "An early watershed towards change in South Africa was sixteen years ago when some five thousand believers from all sides, young and old, of all colors, came together for six days and nights. That was the South African Christian Leadership Assembly. Sam was one of the speakers. And his message from the Lord, in that week, turned the conference around."[29] As preachers and teachers of the word of reconciliation, if our message is from the Lord, it is destined to turn individuals, congregations, and perhaps society around.

QUESTIONS FOR DISCUSSION

1. Why should the narrative about Jesus Christ be the core content of any reconciliation teaching or preaching?

2. Name the different interpretative lenses you bring to Scripture. How do they affect your understanding of the Bible? How do they affect your teaching/preaching or how you receive teaching/preaching? What can you do about their effect?

3. Brainstorm some ways to discover stories and illustrations that would not come across your desk in the course of your normal routine.

4. What style of preaching do you prefer? What style of teaching do you prefer? What style of preaching and/or teaching do you think is most effective in the ministry of reconciliation? Why?

5. In your opinion, does a speaker's own personal life affect the message? Why or why not? What is more important, a righteous life or a right message?

NOTES

1. James Forbes, *The Holy Spirit and Preaching* (Nashville: Abingdon, 1989), 98.
2. Martin Brokenleg, "A Native American Perspective: 'That My People May Live,' " in Christine Marie Smith, *Preaching Justice: Ethnic and Cultural Perspectives* (Cleveland: United Church Press, 1998), 32.
3. James Earl Massey, *The Burdensome Joy of Preaching* (Nashville: Abingdon, 1998), 14.
4. Ibid., 41.
5. Eleazar S. Fernandez, "A Filipino Perspective: 'Unfinished Dream' in the Land of Promise," in Smith, *Preaching Justice,* 63.
6. Jung Young Lee, *Korean Preaching: An Interpretation* (Nashville: Abingdon, 1997), 15.
7. Lucy Atkinson Rose, *Sharing the Word: Preaching in the Roundtable Church* (Louisville: Westminster John Knox, 1997), 129.
8. Brokenleg, "A Native American Perspective," 31.
9. Lee, *Korean Preaching,* 71.
10. Justo L. Gonzalez, "A Hispanic Perspective: By the Rivers of Babylon," in Smith, *Preaching Justice,* 96.
11. For an overview of the Bible and cultural diversity, see Curtiss Paul DeYoung, *Coming Together: The Bible's Message in an Age of Diversity* (Valley Forge, Pa.: Judson, 1995).
12. See James W. English, *Handyman of the Lord: The Life and Ministry of the Rev. William Holmes Borders* (New York: Meredith, 1967), 33–34; quoted in James Earl Massey, *The Responsible Pulpit* (Anderson, Ind.: Warner, 1974), 105–6.
13. Samuel G. Hines, *Experience the Power* (Anderson, Ind.: Warner, 1993, 1995), 24.
14. For more information on the Samaritan concept of the "Taheb" (revealer) see DeYoung, *Coming Together,* 83–84.
15. Gonzalez, "A Hispanic Perspective," 88.
16. Henry Ward Beecher, *Lectures on Preaching* (Glasgow: John S. Marr & Sons, 1872), 6, 7.
17. Phillips Brooks, *Lectures on Preaching* (New York: E. P. Dutton, 1877), 163.
18. Evans E. Crawford with Thomas H. Troeger, *The Hum: Call and Response in African American Preaching* (Nashville: Abingdon, 1995), 22.
19. For more on the ability of Martin Luther King Jr. to preach in interracial settings, see Richard Lischer, *The Preacher King: Martin Luther King Jr. and the Word That Moved America* (New York: Oxford University Press, 1995); and Keith D. Miller, *Voice of Deliverance: The Language of Martin Luther King, Jr. and Its Sources* (New York: Free Press, 1992).
20. Teresa Fry Brown, "An African American Woman's Perspective: Renovating Sorrow's Kitchen," in Smith, *Preaching Justice,* 47.
21. Brokenleg, "A Native American Perspective," 42.
22. David Simon and Edward Burns, *The Corner: A Year in the Life of an Inner-city Neighborhood* (New York: Broadway Books, 1997), 417.
23. From a sermon preached by Curtiss Paul DeYoung on December 21, 1997, at Bethel African Methodist Episcopal Church in Baltimore, audiotape.

24. Beecher, *Lectures on Preaching,* 33.

25. Kelly Miller Smith, *Social Crisis Preaching* (Macon: Mercer University Press, 1984), 99.

26. James Earl Massey, "Thurman's Preaching: Substance and Style," in Henry J. Young, ed., *God and Human Freedom: A Festschrift in Honor of Howard Thurman* (Richmond, Ind.: Friends United Press, 1983), 113.

27. James Earl Massey, *The Sermon in Perspective: A Study of Communication and Charisma* (Anderson, Ind.: Warner, 1976), 105.

28. James Earl Massey also makes this claim in *Designing the Sermon: Order and Movement in Preaching* (Nashville: Abingdon, 1980), 52.

29. Ross Main, speaking at the funeral of Samuel Hines, January 13, 1995, Metropolitan Baptist Church, Washington, D.C., audiotape. Also see Hines, *Experience the Power,* 63. Chapter 5 in this book is adapted from Hines' message.

9

A Godly Explosion That Brings Cohesion

How God Reshapes Us for Reconciliation[1]

SAMUEL GEORGE HINES

AS YOU KNOW BY NOW, I AM A NATIVE SON OF JAMAICA. SEVENTEEN YEARS after being ordained to the Christian ministry, having served as senior pastor for five churches in Jamaica (four of these churches comprised one "circuit" of churches on the island), and having traveled extensively in the British Isles and the United States, I was called to pastor a small church in Washington, D.C. In 1969, after much intense prayer for the Holy Spirit's leading, I answered the call to come to the capital city of the United States.

Just before saying farewell to the magnificent, perennially warm climate of my island home, one of my ministerial colleagues asked me a question that had already been uppermost in my mind. When he heard that my family and I were leaving Jamaica for the United States, he seemed stunned and asked me, "Sam, I hear that you are going to America. What for?"

"To preach, to pastor," I replied.

"Where will you be?" he asked.

"In Washington, D.C.," I answered.

He further pressed the issue by asking, "Why would you do that?"

I replied, "Why? Because the Lord has called me to go there."

With a look of perplexity on his face, he said, "Sam, I don't think that God would ask you to do that. So don't blame him for anything that happens over there."

I am still not sure of all that he meant to imply, but I am thankful to God for the call to come to the United States and the grace to respond positively to this call. After we settled in Washington, D.C., I continually remained before God in prayer. Every time I asked about the purpose for my being in the United States, the answer came in just one word: *reconciliation.*

In this final chapter I summarize some of what has been detailed earlier in this book, as well as expand on what has already been said. I do this in order to press us toward the *practice* of reconciliation. We must allow God to reshape us into proactive ambassadors. My study of the Scriptures, of history, and of the whole body of recorded and developing revelation, points to God's "one-item agenda" that is summed up in one word—*reconciliation.* That item did not change when sin interrupted the order and blessing of God's creation. Reconciliation was and still remains the basis for every action and intervention of God in the affairs that impact humankind. Those persons who acknowledge God as the sovereign ruler of the universe have no option but to witness to the reconciling work of God through Jesus Christ. By taking on human flesh and therefore identifying with the human condition, Jesus, the sinless Son of God, became the only appropriate sacrifice before the Father for the sin of the whole world. His redemptive work on the cross cleared the way for all people to be brought back into a right relationship—reconciliation—with God.

One of the biblical meanings of the word *reconcile* is "to completely change." Reconciliation is not just a matter of a few people backslapping one another or having a few nice social chitchats with some folks against whom they may have a grievance. It is much more than making some social adjustments to one another culturally. Reconciliation goes a long way beyond accommodation or making some well-meaning and usually long overdue acts of reparation. Some or all of these actions may be necessary in various situations of conflict and estrangement, but to reconcile means to change completely, to undergo a radical change in perspective and to see God as well as the people around us from a totally different point of view. The Bible maintains that such a change is imperative for human beings to rightly relate to God and achieve lasting peace with one another.

Reconciliation—The Force

Godly, holistic reconciliation is the only force that has the inherent power to set the world "right-side up" in the areas of separation from God, fractured personal relationships, community and national disruptions, as well as in international arenas of conflict. Dozens or hundreds or even thousands of people meet together at least once a week in local congregations. When intentional reconciliation across all lines and barriers does not become a practiced lifestyle in these communities, we end up with large conglomerates of people who care little for one another, and therefore no true unity of spirit exists. Reconciliation is God's plan to change individual attitudes, perspectives, and behaviors so that there will be, corporately, nationally, and internationally, "peace among those whom he favors" (Luke 2:14). It bears repeating that, until we as individuals change on the inside, there will be no lasting change in the corporate, national, or international scene. Reconciliation is God's plan for revealing and releasing new and vital possibilities of empowerment for all of us in our struggles and frustrations.

Reconciliation between human beings and their Creator reverses the effect of sin objectively, that is, from God's perspective. This explosion of reconciliation literally reverses the effect of sin on the human race by announcing to the whole world that we can *now*—not in a distant millennium—be restored to God's original plan of unity for all creation. We can enjoy communion with the all-powerful and all-wise God. This internal force then enables us to embrace one another in fellowship as we revel in the creativity and splendor of our diversity. God made a great, beautiful, and productive world and looked upon it and "saw that it was good" (Genesis 1:25). Next, God made man and saw that he was "very good" (1:31). Then God said, "It is not good that the man should be alone" (2:18). God saw that man could develop into an egotist so wrapped up in himself that he would become a diminishing personality. So God made woman and thus established community. That is what maleness and femaleness are all about, not the obsession with sexuality that pervades so much of our world today. Community! Cohesion! People—men and women—are about community. This cornerstone of God's plan for the universe went into effect for us countless eons before any philosophers, psychologists, or sociologists emerged on the scene.

Sin, our disobedience to God, causes us to fall short of the Almighty's expectations for us. It results in the drastic cancellation of the arrangement that God put in place so that all humankind could live in close communion with their God. The Almighty's provision of reconciliation removes the inevitable curse of our separation from God and the spiritual death that sin deserves, "for the wages of sin is death" (Romans 6:23). This vertical reconciliation with God empowers us to move into horizontal reconciliation with one another. All of the people of God need to continually allow the Spirit of God to break down our stubborn wills and our know-it-all attitudes. Then God will remake us from the inside out so that we progressively become more like Jesus, the Lord of our lives. Our yardstick for ethical, moral, and spiritual living is not any law or any other person, it is *Jesus Christ himself*. As Paul admonished the Philippians, we must pursue our lives: "Forgetting what lies behind and straining forward to what lies ahead, I press on toward the goal for the prize of the heavenly call of God in Christ Jesus" (Philippians 3:13–14).

A Profile of Biblical Reconciliation

Godly reconcilers promote and practice reconciliation from a biblical, holistic perspective. They recognize and believe that reconciliation is God's one-item agenda. As the apostle Paul wrote:

> But now in Christ Jesus you who were once far off have been brought near by the blood of Christ. For he is our peace; in his flesh he has made both groups into one and has broken down the dividing wall, that is, the hostility between us. . . . that he might create in himself one new humanity in place of the two, thus making peace, and might reconcile both groups to God in one body through the cross, thus putting to death that hostility through it (Ephesians 2:13–16).

Not everyone who uses the term *reconciliation* speaks from the same point of view as Paul. Therefore, my wife and I have developed the following profile that lists some of the foundations of biblical, holistic reconciliation.

1. God is the *author* of reconciliation. We human beings only carry out the reconciling process that God has initiated.

2. Genuine reconciliation begins first between God and human beings through the atonement of God's Son, Jesus Christ. The reconciled are then empowered to become agents of reconciliation.

3. Godly, holistic reconciliation calls us to center our lives in recognition of the sovereignty of God and the lordship of Jesus Christ.

4. Reconciliation brings about the restoration of right relationships between God and humankind and between individuals of both genders, all ages, races, cultures, levels of society, nationalities, political beliefs, and religious persuasions.

5. The dictionary defines reconciliation as bringing together again in love or friendship. The Bible defines reconciliation as changing completely in order to fit. The sacrificial redemption of Jesus established that godly reconciliation includes all people, whether they have been friends before a given circumstance or not.

6. Reconciliation, the work of God in human hearts, must be based on the building of personal relationships before it can be effective programmatically.

7. Reconciliation moves us from personal piety to public witness, which challenges our own integrity and the power blocs around us, whether they are religious, intellectual, political, economic, or media-related.

8. Reconciliation among human beings necessitates a cycle of mutual forgiveness and repentance. Each is a key that opens the door for the other to be expressed.

9. Reconciliation is a work, a ministry, of unconditional love and unbiased networking.

10. Sincere efforts at reconciliation must always be approached with the conviction that it is not just desirable or probable, but possible.

11. Reconciliation and eventual peace will not happen if any of the parties involved in a dispute seek or desire to win an arrogant victory.

12. Reconciliation goes beyond accommodation, integration, and conflict resolution to a reorientation of our perspectives, a rejection of biased thinking, and an intentional decision to maintain peaceful relationships.

13. Reconciliation brings people to maintain a focus of mutuality, with each person or group learning from and building up the other.

14. Reconciliation does not allow for any posture or attitude of paternalism either inherent or expressed.

15. Reconciliation between groups of persons will often require the impacting of governmental agencies, interfacing with lawmakers, and advocating for the helpless, so as to ensure impartiality in the

systems of law and order, as well as justice for the disenfranchised and the dispossessed.

16. Reconciliation demands recognition of and respect for the inherent dignity of every human being and a complete departure from the tendency or desire to belittle anyone for any reason.

17. Reconciliation, at any given time, can be targeted to but not isolated around any single area of living, because it relates to and impacts all of life.

18. Reconciliation brings about unity, not uniformity. It embraces unity in diversity. This is a compelling, convicting, and convincing message of a radical transformation in our intellectual perceptions and societal expectations.

19. Reconciliation is a radical word that describes a revolutionary process for building or reestablishing peaceful relations between estranged persons.

20. Reconciliation, if it is to be lasting, requires us to be continually involved in intercessory prayer, across-the-lines interactions, and activities of humble service to others.

Jesus—The Propellant and the Glue

God sent Jesus to this planet to take on human form and bear the burden of human sin so that he could become the effective instrument of reconciliation between divinity and humanity. Jesus took upon himself the eternal punishment that we had coming to us. Now, since he died for us, we can abide in him and partake of his life-giving Spirit. We can live in and be filled with the Spirit of the resurrected Christ forevermore. Sin need not dominate or destroy us, for we are covered with the righteousness of God. We overcome, not in our own strength, but by the blood of the Lamb "that was slain from the creation of the world" (Revelation 13:8, NIV). That is how God initiated reconciliation. Paul wrote in Romans 5:10–11, "If while we were enemies, we were reconciled to God through the death of his Son, much more surely, having been reconciled, will we be saved by his life. But more than that, we even boast in God through our Lord Jesus Christ, through whom we have now received reconciliation."

The problem of estrangement and separation between individuals is dealt with in the New Testament in only one way—that God has reconciled all people in Jesus. In his living and by his dying, Jesus broke down the wall of partition between persons of all races, classes, cultures, genders, and age groups. At the foot of the cross of Jesus, we are all on level ground. The epistle to the Ephesians is a great resource for any study of godly, holistic reconciliation. It provides a clear message that God has a one-item agenda, which is, "to bring all things in heaven and on earth together under one head, even Christ" (Ephesians 1:10, NIV). The declaration here is that it is God's transcending, superior purpose to create a christocentric universe.

In his second letter to the Corinthians, the apostle Paul declares that "Christ's love compels us" (2 Corinthians 5:14, NIV). We are told over and over again that Christ's love compels us, indwells us, and impels us. We also need to grasp and hold on to another exciting concept of the significant word translated from the Greek language to our English Bibles to mean compel or constrain. The word in the original language is *synechei*. Besides the other meanings, the word also carries the sense of cohesiveness, or holding together. So the love of Christ holds us together. We are held together as a community already reconciled, always reconcilable, and commissioned to be a reconciling force in the world. The love of Jesus causes an explosive change to happen within us that enables us to develop this new cohesiveness. Only the Almighty God could create such a rational paradox! We can stick together no matter what the prevailing circumstances or philosophies around us may be, for the love of Christ within us causes us to hold fast to one another.

If church polity, church programs, and church growth do not include godly, holistic reconciliation at the core of their plans and projects, they are doomed to fall into the same pit of nonfulfillment in which the unredeemed find themselves on a constantly recurring basis. The people who meet together to seek fellowship in places of worship are not just an aggregate of individuals who provide their leaders with a cause for bragging. They do not constitute a necklace of diamonds, with each entity being sanctified in order to remain separate, satisfied, and petrified. Because they are reconciled to God, the people of God are called to take the message of salvation and reconciliation to the ends of the earth, beginning right where they are. They are ambassadors of reconciliation. Whenever congregants become merely a nice crowd of saved "look-alike, smell-alike, sound-alike" people, sitting in comfortable pews, they will not be ready or able to impact the society around them and bring about the kind of change God desires to see in this world.

The thrust of the biblical message about reconciliation is neither any individual's hobbyhorse or a seasonal fad that the people of God may follow if and when they feel like it. No! Reconciliation is the primary agenda of God and therefore must be a central focus for the universal church, the body of Christ. God has a powerful means of bringing us together. Whether we are Jew or Gentile, enslaved or free, young or old, educated or unlearned, churched or unchurched, religious or irreligious, rich or poor, powerful or powerless, we are all one in Christ Jesus. Whether we live or have our origins in Africa, Asia, America (North or South), Australia, Europe, or an island of the sea, we are all one in Christ Jesus. Regardless of skin color, culture, gender, class, or denomination, we are all one in Christ Jesus. God's Word puts us all together by stating clearly that "all have sinned and fall short of the glory of God" (Romans 3:23).

Then the Bible goes on to declare that we were reconciled, *all* of us, unto God by Jesus Christ. This brings a whole new focus to Christian ministry. We have to let people know that, in spite of the escalation of violence and the seeming enthronement of evil, the miracle of reconciliation has already taken place through Jesus. By the witness of our lives and our lips, we then have to help others understand how they can accept Jesus into their lives and live out this liberating and unifying blessing for themselves. No individual can make another person or group become reconciled to others. We humbly and passionately speak the message that God has already completed the reconciling work in Jesus. We then encourage others, by the transparent integrity of our own lifestyle, to make a commitment to apply this truth to their own lives.

A Portrait of Godly Reconcilers

The apostle Paul offered an eloquent description of the godly reconciler when he wrote: "If anyone is in Christ, there is a new creation: everything old has passed away; see, everything has become new! All this is from God, who reconciled us to himself through Christ, and has given us the ministry of reconciliation" (2 Corinthians 5:17–18). The following portrait of godly reconcilers is a helpful checklist for our ministries. This list includes many of the attributes necessary for ambassadors of reconciliation.

1. Reconcilers must know, understand, and practice the two great commandments: " 'You shall love the Lord your God with all your heart, and with all your soul, and with all your mind, and with all

your strength.' The second is this, 'You shall love your neighbor as yourself.' There is no other commandment greater than these" (Mark 12:30–31).

2. Reconcilers must first be in a right relationship with God and at peace within themselves before attempting to help other people to make or keep peace.

3. Reconcilers should seek to create a healthy atmosphere of open "carefrontation"[2] rather than adversarial confrontation. People on both sides of a disagreement need to pledge not to gain points or win a battle, but to save and develop personhood and relationships.

4. Reconcilers are facilitators. They cannot effect reconciliation without the intentional commitment of the parties involved.

5. Reconcilers do not seek to spare themselves or save face for themselves. They have to be prepared, like their example, Jesus, to be wounded in the conflict.

6. Reconcilers will only be minimally effective unless they develop a lifestyle of prayer and communion with God, as they seek wisdom in all their undertakings.

7. Reconcilers, in order to be credible, must model reconciling behaviors in their homes, businesses, communities, churches, schools, and all other places.

8. Reconcilers do not blame other people for the symptoms of alienation. They seek solutions to the causes of estrangements and take responsibility to initiate actions that will eliminate the problematic situations.

9. Reconcilers do not speak the language of separation from polarized platforms if they seriously intend to help people to find and maintain peace.

10. Reconcilers must be prepared to deal with frustration without giving up hope for positive resolutions between opposing individuals or groups. The strength and lasting quality of reconciliation lies in the commitment of the reconcilers and the reconciled to stick with the process.

11. Reconcilers must be strong, courageous, and unwavering in their support of justice while they remain compassionate in their dealings with both victims and wrongdoers.

12. Reconcilers have to be willing to move out of their accustomed places (comfort zones) and groups (labeled boxes) in order to reach

people and influence situations in places and circumstances where others will not venture.

13. Reconcilers need to develop the skills to become involved, when necessary, in advocacy between the rich and the poor, the educated and the uneducated, the young and the old, the powerful and the powerless, the native and the immigrant, as well as between the churched and the unchurched.

14. Reconcilers, recognizing their areas of competence and limitations, should work in areas where they can be effective in bringing about de-escalation of tension, disagreement, and violence. Lack of knowledge or misinformation can cause exacerbation and further splintering in already troubled situations.

15. Reconcilers must themselves willingly acknowledge that the beauty and lasting quality of reconciliation lies in the pooled strength that diverse groups bring together in unified efforts.

16. Reconcilers must help others, while they themselves, under God, willingly build and cross bridges between people who are in conflict everywhere—children and parents, church or parachurch groups, different racial and/or cultural groups, males and females, people of different age groups, or persons of varying political and religious persuasions.

17. Reconcilers must practice and teach unconditional love and unlimited forgiveness, recognizing that our forgiveness from God is conditioned on our forgiveness of others. "Our Father. . . . forgive us our debts, as we also have forgiven our debtors. . . . For if you forgive others their trespasses, your heavenly Father will also forgive you; but if you do not forgive others, neither will your Father forgive your trespasses" (Matthew 6:9,12,14–15).

18. Reconcilers must spread the good news of the gospel that God's power and love have already broken down all of the barriers that divide people. We, the people of God, are Christ's ambassadors of reconciliation.

Reconciliation—Its Sense and Strength

In terms of human relationships, reconciliation is the most expensive and explosive undertaking in the world. In spite of that, however, godly reconcilers must make intentional and sustained efforts to establish and keep reconciled relationships with all persons. This is the only basis upon which we can effect lasting personal, national, or international relief from the devastating results arising out of bitterness, discrimination, exploitation, estrangement, injustice, racial prejudice, and war. This is the only means by which we will ever experience mutual caring, nonexploitative cooperation, unexplainable joy, true liberation, and unconditional love. Without godly, holistic reconciliation, we have no hope of escaping wholesale, mutual annihilation of one another here on planet earth. Without this ingredient, neither church projects, educational, governmental, private or social programs, legislative or other mandated propositions, or high-level caucuses will effectively change the way we act and react toward one another for any sustained period of time. The people of God are entrusted with the responsibility to think reconciliation, preach it humbly (but with authority), and literally model that lifestyle before the people around them, so that others may recognize and accept it as a viable option for living. The job is not easy, but we have the resources of the mighty and eternal God at our disposal.

The battles within and between us are destroying the basic units that make up our society. If we ignore the disunity of the parts, the whole—the composite structure—will be faulty and unsound. The search for unity in diversity must acknowledge and seek after possibilities for those expressions of "alikeness" that bind us together in Jesus Christ. At the same time, we must maintain the highest respect for the opinions of other persons who do not look, speak, or believe like us. We view one another, the world around us, and truth through a number of different lenses, such as culture, tradition, historical heritage, prejudices, preferences, sectarian loyalties, political affiliations, and even personal arrogance. However, since God is the Father of us all and Jesus died for us all, we stand on the common ground of spiritual kinship that should flow out into unity among us as individuals. If we continue to disregard and scoff at all efforts for reconciliation, regardless of who may initiate them, our fears and distrust of one another will continue to cast dark shadows over our homes, our communities, and our world.

When we are reconciled to God, we are entrusted with the word of reconciliation. Our function, as reconcilers, is controlled by divine design, not by human desires. Our reconciliation to God means that godly fear will instruct our ethics, manage our morals, correct our conduct, and regulate us in right living. This is the same "fear," or godly reverence, that prompts us to holiness, moves us to mercy, and insists on our purity of heart while it holds us together with other people in peace. The fear of the Lord pumps energy and urgency into our ministry and keeps on reminding us that we stand in transparency before the all-seeing eyes of God. So, although we fear God—that is, hold God in highest reverence—we do not have to be afraid. Those who fear God have nothing else to fear.

As human beings, one of our greatest problems is fear of people. Many persons hesitate or refuse to participate in reconciling encounters because they are afraid. Some say they are afraid:

- of being used as a "doormat" by others
- of being perceived as compromising their stand
- of linking with "those people"
- because it has never been done that way before
- because it is too late in the relationship for any good to result

These reasons may be given by individuals, or they may be referenced by groups. To be emancipated, "people who experience the power of God must find in that divine force the courage to cross human boundaries and express unrestrained love for other people, to the glory of God."[3] We need to focus on this truth in our thinking, because it will free us up to stop concentrating on the things that divide us or those that we think make us special. We need to stop finding little private corners for ourselves in the will of God. We all share the same Lord, and we can all be lifted by a common force to new levels of life.

Jesus told his disciples, "Very truly, I tell you, the one who believes in me will also do the works that I do and, in fact, will do greater works than these, because I am going to the Father. I will do whatever you ask in my name, so that the Father may be glorified in the Son" (John 14:12–13). One of the most powerful forces available to the biblical reconciler is the power of prayer. Any attempt to enter into godly, holistic reconciling processes must be saturated with continuous intercessory prayer. The reconciler must be able to share the pain of the struggle as well as the joy of ultimate resolution. When we allow God to grace us with the character of a reconciler and we truly understand the process of reconciliation (and it is a process, not just a happening), we will be able to adopt the following, "Strategies for Reconciliation" as we work with God to bring peace among estranged people wherever and whenever we can.

Strategies for Reconciliation

Any strategy for reconciliation begins with prayer—"Finally. . . . pray for us that the message of the Lord may spread rapidly and be honored" (2 Thessalonians 3:1, NIV). We must—PRAY! PRAY! PRAY! PRAY!

PRAY! We know that God, as the author of reconciliation, reconciles us and empowers us to become agents of reconciliation. As ambassadors of reconciliation, we recognize that reconciliation will not happen just because it is right, but that the process involves a lifetime commitment to change personally and to encourage others to seek peace in all human interactions. The following list represents a number of strategies that have proven to be helpful.

1. To be effective reconcilers, we must recognize that a problem of estrangement exists and has damaging effects on individuals and society.

2. Reconciliation encounters cannot be conducted like court trials. There must not be any aim to establish guilt and determine punishment for one person or group while rewarding the other for good behavior.

3. In horizontal reconciliation (between individuals and nations) the motivation and aim of the reconciler is to guide all the people involved into recognizing how they may have contributed to the controversy and how resolution may be mutually attained.

4. Confession and repentance of damaging attitudes about self, others, and life's situations are all parts of the vital fabric of reconciliation.

5. All persons who find themselves in conflicting interactions have to be led to relinquish the attitude of blaming others for the existing estrangement and be willing to initiate actions and dialogue (face-to-face whenever possible) that will lead to increased understanding, restored communication, the settlement of differences, and lasting reconciliation.

6. Contending parties must be stimulated toward mutual repentance and forgiveness—with reparation, restoration, and restitution, if indicated—so that they can be freed up for unified action toward building reconciled relationships and restoring wholeness to life.

7. If genuine and lasting reconciliation is to be realized, the estranged persons must experience a radical change in perspective toward one another so that arrogance, bigotry, discrimination, and one-upmanship become intolerable to them. This change must be based on the principles of unconditional love outlined in 1 Corinthians 13:1–13.

8. The reconciling process must provide opportunities for people to learn to treasure one another, in spite of differences of age, class, culture,

educational achievement, gender, political persuasion, race, skin color, or denominational affiliation.

9. The reconciler usually has to help the people who have been newly reconciled to understand ways in which they can facilitate the new walk of unity they have embraced.

10. Arrangements must be made for newly reconciled individuals to be accountable to and supported by others so that they will maintain the impetus of the mutual decisions made toward resolution of the conflict. This refers to family or church members, economic, political, and racial groups, as well as national enclaves.

11. It is sometimes helpful to have symbols of reconciliation at hand to dramatize the substantive meaning of a covenant of reconciliation. These symbols must not, however, take the place of continuing and relevant action toward the maintenance of a reconciled relationship.

12. The decisions, policies, programs, or laws that are decided upon in the reconciling process must be mutually beneficial to all persons involved.

13. Based on our recognition of the sovereignty of God, our pursuit of biblical reconciliation will be based on the realization that our similarities always outweigh our dissimilarities. In the reconciling process, people are strongly encouraged to focus on their "alikeness" and relinquish their prejudicial and stereotypic thinking of others.

14. Serious efforts at reconciliation will allow for networking in all kinds of cross-cultural, cross-generational, interdenominational, and interracial experiences as we practice openly and boldly the work of building reconciled communities.

15. In many areas of relational strife, children and youth should be included in discussions about, planning for, and implementation of reconciling interactions.

16. The reconciling process always necessitates that estranged people work together on words and attitudes that trigger contention, fear, and hatred, by bringing them out into the open. They then work together to eliminate or modify and translate these terms into mutually acceptable language.

17. The existence of "ghettos" will always continue the evil of alienation. To bring about reconciliation in our communities, cities, and

nations, intentional efforts must be made to eliminate these pockets of isolation.

18. Reconciling activities require patience. Since polarization does not usually happen overnight, it is unrealistic to expect that reconciliation will be a swift process.

19. In today's world, since we live in a global village formation, reconciling processes for communities and nations must include media input.

20. Reconcilers must get beyond promoting, teaching, and preaching the principles of reconciliation. They must practice them.

21. Our homes and churches should be the primary arenas in which to model the process of reconciliation.

Breaking and Making

Our church fellowship in Washington, D.C., has maintained several outreach ministries for many years. One of these is a ministry to poor and homeless people known as the Urban Breakfast Ministry. At this time, an average of three hundred people come into the church every morning, Monday through Friday, to worship and praise God, hear the invitation of the gospel, and eat a meal together. The meal is followed by myriad activities that impact life. They include sharing burdens, giving and receiving counseling in connection with family and other relational disputes, providing a safe environment and nonjudgmental atmosphere for people to unload their guilt when necessary, gaining help to negotiate the bureaucracy for various reasons, participating in literacy and job counseling sessions, and many other necessary activities. The people who come hear about and are stimulated to respond to the claims of redemption and the call to rehabilitation and reempowerment. We also sponsor and house an after-school learning center for at-risk children in the community. These children receive academic and religious instruction, mentoring, and nurturing from kindergarten through their high school and college years.

When one understands reconciliation, none of these individuals is regarded as a bum or derelict or is given any other derogatory title. We respect the adults as brothers and sisters and the children as "our children." People from the powerful echelons on Capitol Hill, from many church denominations, from business organizations in the metro area, as well as youth and adults from around the nation and across the world have come to "walk with us" in these ministries. They come to serve, learn, and share. Often they find that they receive more blessings than they give. The powerful serve the powerless in this setting, and the powerless share their wisdom with the powerful. This is a start in the reconciling process for many on both ends of the spectrum.

The Bible says, "There will always be poor people in the land. Therefore I command you to be openhanded toward your brothers and toward the poor and needy in your land" (Deuteronomy 15:11, NIV). Some people deal with this class of person in three different categories—the brother, the poor, and the needy. This is based on an erroneous understanding of the Scriptures. Careful study reveals that all three terms are synonyms for the same people. Nowhere in the Bible do the writers refer to people in need as bums or rascals. When we are reconciled to God, we see all people, including those who are poor and needy, as God sees them. They are our brothers and sisters made in God's image. Homeless and other indigent persons need more than a handout, they need a "handup." The vast majority of them need the stimulus of knowing that someone cares enough to help them learn how to fit in with God's plan for their lives. Then they go on from there to utilize the help available to rediscover their families and become contributing members in the society around them.

William Shakespeare wrote many centuries ago that all of us have our exits and entrances on the stage of life. Persons in need must find exits from abandonment, depression, desertion, disappointment, crime, poverty, abuse of many kinds, as well as myriad other cycles of ego-assassination to which many are exposed, sometimes from very early in life. They need people who are willing to help them find entrances into the good life without the patronization that only further lowers their self-esteem. Godly, holistic reconciliation is the key to resolution in these situations, because every person is recognized as being a son or daughter of God and is therefore treated as being of equal worth. The apostle Paul wrote, "From now on, therefore, we regard no one from a human point of view; even though we once knew Christ from a human point of view, we know him no longer in that way" (2 Corinthians 5:16). I have witnessed the transformation of hundreds of lives through this ministry.

Church growth must continue, but that growth must involve persons who have the mind-set of no longer living unto themselves and no longer see people as identified by biased thinking. When we are reconciled to

God and we understand reconciliation more clearly, we get beyond all prevailing barriers, such as nationalism and racism, although there is nothing wrong with honoring, knowing, and preserving one's nationhood or race. We must put culture and heredity in their proper perspectives so that we do not yield to the crippling assumptions and limitations to which bigotry can lead us. If you are still embracing negative or belittling ideas about other people, you are still living as the unreconciled—still living unto yourself outside the grace of God.

True Liberation

Reconciliation brings godly empowerment. It frees you from the bondage of living according to other people's opinions of you. You no longer live at the mercy of your temptations and your frustrations, for you are held together on the inside by Christ's love. Because of this power of love, Jesus Christ voluntarily shed the glory of his heavenly kingdom and came to earth in human flesh so that he could be identified with us as human beings. This same eternal and all-embracing love impelled Jesus Christ to die for sinners. The omnipotent power of the Godhead—Father, Son, and Holy Spirit—brought Jesus Christ back to life and out of the tomb so that you and I might have a right to union and eternal life with God. The incarnation, life, crucifixion, resurrection, and glorification of Jesus were triggered by his obedience to God the Father and his love for us with the purpose of making it possible for us to be reconciled to God—"We know love by this, that he laid down his life for us" (1 John 3:16). Jesus ascended back to heaven and remains continually at God's throne of grace making intercession for us.

So then, if we embrace the sacrifice of Jesus, we can be held together by his love, both inside of ourselves and with the people around us. Jesus Christ made it possible for all of us to live together in peace in spite of the traditional, historical, and sociological pressures that tend to keep us apart. Prevalent cliques, partisan groups, academic divisions, and religious labels inevitably lead to the fracturing of relationships, with each group determined to prove they are better than the other. Society seems determined to make us into enemies, to alienate us, and then pulverize us while we are looking hatefully and suspiciously at one another. But reconciled people have had a radical change in their hearts and minds. They have come in repentance, with broken hearts before God, and have been made new. This is true liberation.

We all need to lock into the divine perspective, which is to "regard no one from a human point of view" (2 Corinthians 5:16). The people of God should not and must not persist in judging or relating to people by worldly standards. In a very real sense, reconciled people have relocated, internally. They no longer emphasize whether they happen to reside in the suburbs or in the inner city. They no longer focus on whether they belong to the haves or have-nots. Reconciled people live in Christ Jesus—that is true relocation. The apostle Paul made a passionate plea to Christians in Rome when he spoke these words that echo down the corridors of time: "I appeal to you therefore, brothers and sisters, by the mercies of God, to present your bodies as a living sacrifice, holy and acceptable to God, which is your spiritual worship. Do not be conformed to this world, but be transformed by the renewing of your minds, so that you may discern what is the will of God—what is good and acceptable and perfect" (Romans 12:1–2). Only God can create within us the radical, complete change that we need to experience in order to be reconciled. Only then can we be empowered as authentic agents of reconciliation to the people around us. God must break us in order to make us into who we are called to be.

Let us look again at 2 Corinthians 5:17: "Everything old has passed away; see, everything has become new!" This refers to people who have been reconciled to God, but it seems that even we keep forgetting that word "everything." We black pastors in predominantly black churches have to constantly remind our people that the world is not composed of only black people. White pastors in predominantly white churches have to constantly remind their congregants that the world is not made up only of white people. The same thing applies to fellowships that are composed of Asian, Middle-Eastern, Hispanic, Native American, or any other predominant ethnic group. Our ethnicity does not dictate our character or intrinsic worth. We should constantly remind ourselves of the very old saying: "There is so much good in the worst of us, and so much bad in the best of us, that it hardly behooves any of us to talk about the rest of us." *All* of us are reconciled, not on the basis of race, but on the basis of grace. That grace is not in a culture or a system but in a person—Jesus Christ.

It is necessary to make another very important observation at this point. You will notice that the Bible never says that God is reconciled. It never says so, because that would be a wrong and blasphemous statement. To be reconciled means to be completely changed and reconciled to God. God is immutable—he never changes! If God were to change at all, God would no longer be God! God does not change to suit our whims and fancies. God does not adjust to our cultural and situational patterns. Let us always remember that we need to change, and since we cannot do that all by ourselves, God has done it for us in Jesus Christ.

A Living Love That Lasts

The theme of reconciliation resides deep in my heart. I was born in a small town on the tiny island of Jamaica in the West Indies. First the Spaniards and then the British came to that island, conquered it by their superior armaments, and then brought in slave and indentured laborers to work the sugar, coconut, and banana plantations. Neither of the invaders came to reconcile anyone to anything. They came to get rich. The entire native Indian population died out from diseases brought in by the foreigners or by the physical abuse they suffered. As the decades passed, people from most of the nations on earth came and settled in Jamaica for one reason or another. I am a descendant of the polyglot mixture of bloodlines in that island. Our island motto is, "Out of many, one people." Maybe we caught a glimpse of the need for reconciliation a little earlier than some other people.

I do not have the energy or inclination to remain bitter about this history or to hate any of the nationals involved. The main reason for my attitude is that I experienced this radical change of salvation from my sins and reconciliation with God right on that little island. As I mentioned at the beginning of this book, the very first thing that God did for me was to give me love in my heart for a lady who had lied about me. Ever since that time, God has put in my heart an unconditional love for all people—particularly those who hurt me and try to give me a hard time. I love them because I have no right or option to do anything else.

Whenever we consider God's reconciling work, one of the features that comes into view is the quality of unconditional love. "For God so loved the world that he gave his only Son, so that everyone who believes in him may not perish but may have eternal life" (John 3:16). There is a certain feature to love that is known as endearment.[4] It implies the quality of "treasuring" or "valuing." It indicates love's perception—how one sees or views or regards the person one loves. Although the word *endearment* cannot be found in the Bible, this quality reflects God's love. The Scriptures tell us that when we accept the atoning work of Jesus for our own personal salvation, the love of God fills our hearts. When this happens, this quality of endearment becomes a feature of our own lifestyle, because we see people from God's point of view. Every redeemed child of God should read, memorize, and pray for the grace to put into practice all the aspects of love that are outlined in 1 Corinthians 13. (See "A Personal Inventory" in the Supplemental Workbook Section.)

Obedience to the Vision

When I relocated to Washington, D.C., from Jamaica, I was under the call of God to make reconciliation the pivotal focus of my ministry. As always, I sought God's guidance in order to know how to share this vision with the people under my pastoral leadership. I was led to use Paul's letter to the Ephesians and saturate both them and myself in this teaching. For eighteen consecutive months I preached from that book. In addition, we went on retreats, did workshops, and had Bible studies centered around the truths in Ephesians. Of course, we prayed and fasted. Then we prayed and fasted some more. Little by little, God's purpose for us was revealed, and doors of ministry opened. The entire congregation worked corporately and in small groups to develop a mission statement to which I referred earlier. This became our guideline for worship and ministry projects. The statement reads:

> We are ambassadors for Christ in the Nation's Capital, committed to be a totally open, evangelistic, metropolitan, caring fellowship of believers. To this end we are being discipled in a community of Christian faith, centered in the love of Jesus Christ and administered by the Holy Spirit. We are covenanted to honor God, obey His Word, celebrate His grace, and demonstrate a lifestyle of servanthood. Accordingly, we seek to proclaim and offer to the world a full-cycle ministry of reconciliation and wholeness.

The first question people began to ask was, "How do we practice this?" Then God sent us a man who came into my life as a covenant brother, into the church as a leader, and into the community as a pacesetter and an agent of change. God put us together as a team. Beginning with a small group, we put hands, hearts, and feet to our ministry proclamations of the reconciling grace of God. The work grew, supported only by volunteer workers and backed by private financial donors. God sent people from every walk of life and from every Christian persuasion to serve with us and to be served by us. Many lives are still being transformed through this ministry on a daily basis.

145

Christians can work together harmoniously in ministry even if their doctrines are in conflict. The linking of our fellowship with that of a prestigious, uptown church, for working out this ministry demonstrates the truth that networking in ministry is always a positive factor, leading to cohesiveness among God's people. On the other hand, dogma often causes controversy and divisiveness. The two preachers and their wives got together, and members of the two congregations met and got to know one another. All of us were reconciled believers who made intentional decisions to be reconciled to one another. We simply set about seeing how we could help our people understand the biblical precepts of reconciliation and apply them to their daily living. In neither congregation did all, or even a majority of the members, welcome this "intrusion" into their comfortable, maintenance-oriented fellowship. But small cadres from both, under God, initiated a reconciling ministry. Those ministries remain to this time and continue to bring people back to redemption, reformation, renewal, and reempowerment. As the word of reconciliation continued to be heralded from these and increasing numbers of pulpits, the number of supporters grew and other church fellowships in the metro area began to take up the banner. God has demonstrated over and over again that nothing is too difficult, because "what is impossible for mortals is possible for God" (Luke 18:27).

As Christian ambassadors of reconciliation, we do not stand "anxiously on the sidelines, waiting to see what is going to happen in the world."[5] We have God's one-item agenda in hand. We pursue it aggressively, because God has given us a mandate to be messengers and ministers of reconciliation. The church of Jesus Christ must lead the world in this proclamation and not become a reflection of the status quo. Christ's ambassadors must move beyond cultural appropriateness, political correctness, and social accommodation, declaring the full gospel to all people.

A most compelling task faces each of us as we enter the twenty-first century. That task is to live out the reconciling process. Reconciliation is an *action* word, a today word. We must do more than promote godly reconciliation; we must practice it. *If you cannot find a model, be one.* Godly principles of reconciliation can become practical and lasting realities in our world, wherever that world encompasses—our hearts, our homes, our churches, our communities, our cities, our nation, and our world. Just as "faith without deeds is dead" (James 2:26, NIV), so testimony about reconciliation without practice is hypocrisy. We cannot, we must not, be content only with making peace; we must resolve to work untiringly to keep the peace. Our bridge building cannot be allowed to become an end in itself, we must be willing to cross the bridges that we build. No thinking Christian can settle for less than the maximum involvement in God's one-item agenda—*reconciliation!*

QUESTIONS FOR DISCUSSION

1. How does God reshape us for the ministry of reconciliation? Name as many ways as you can.

2. Select two or three statements from "A Profile of Biblical Reconciliation." Expand on what is being said. How has this proven true in your life?

3. Take a second look at "A Portrait of Godly Reconcilers." Which statements on this list affirm who you are at this point in time? Which statements identify areas of growth?

4. Reread the "Strategies for Reconciliation." Which of these apply to you personally, to your church, or to your city? How can you implement any of these strategies in the next few weeks, the next few months, the next year? What is the role of prayer?

5. Contemplate the relationship between love and obedience in the ministry of reconciliation. What are your thoughts?

NOTES

1. The main text of this chapter is excerpted from a message given by Dr. Samuel G. Hines at the first National Church Growth Conference, which was held in Turro, Virginia, in 1985. Other speakers at the conference included Dr. Paul Yonggi Cho, South Korea; the late Dr. Richard Halverson, United States Senate chaplain; and Dr. Robert Schuller, Crystal Cathedral.

   The profiles on "Godly, Holistic Reconciliation," "Godly Reconcilers," and "Strategies for Reconciliation" were first developed by Dr. Hines and his wife during their interactions with estranged groups in South Africa during the 1970s. The content was expanded as they continued (and Mrs. Hines continues) to counsel and mentor polarized family members, employers and employees, as well as church leaders and the people under their care.

2. David Augsburger, *Caring Enough to Confront* (Scottdale, Pa.: Herald Press, 1973, 1981).

3. Samuel G. Hines, *Experience the Power* (Anderson, Ind.: Warner, 1993, 1995), 80.

4. See ibid., 79.

5. Ibid., 85.

Reconciliation
Is an Action Word

DEVELOPED BY SAMUEL AND DALINETA HINES

A Personal Inventory

THE FOLLOWING CHALLENGE, BASED ON 1 CORINTHIANS 13, PROVIDES A way for you to periodically check on yourself to discover if you have progressed in the area of experiencing and demonstrating the unconditional (*agape*) love that Jesus modeled for us here on earth. Reconciling efforts will be ineffective and short-lived if this basic ingredient is absent.

LOVE—*AGAPE*—(unconditional love that goes beyond erotic or family love) is the basis of our liberation from sin and of the ministry of biblical reconciliation.

Do your first inventory as soon as you finish reading this book. Then do two more inventories at three-month intervals after doing the first one. Keep notes on your progress or lack of it (be totally honest at all times) and seek constant help from God and spiritually sensitive persons as your needs indicate.

To find your average, divide your total by 18. Do not be upset if you do not make perfect 10 point scores. (You would be a very rare person if you did.) The key here is to recognize the areas of your need and present yourself to God for breaking, remaking, and reshaping. The Holy Spirit is still working on every one of us to bring us to the measure of Christ Jesus and make us into vessels fit for the Master's use.

Each day or each week, choose an area in which you feel a need for God's help in making a breakthrough in loving. Pray specifically for deliverance and help in these areas. Then ask God to show you how you can move intentionally from prayer to action in living out your new-found ability to forgive, repent, and love.

On a scale of 1 (lowest) to 10 (highest) make an honest rating of yourself in the following areas:

THEME	VERSE	RATING 1	RATING 2	RATING 3
1. Transparent Lifestyle— Do I walk my talk?	1			
2. Religious Life—Go beyond speaking and gifting	2			
3. Living a Life of Sacrificial Servanthood	3			
4. Patience	4			
5. Gentleness	4			
6. Humility	4			
7. Courtesy	5			
8. Selflessness	5			
9. Self-control	5			
10. Endlessly Forgiving	5			
11. Rejoicing Only in Truth	6			
12. Consistency in Caring	7			
13. Consistency in Trusting	7			
14. Consistency in Hoping	7			
15. Unswerving Love	7			
16. Recognizing Limitations	8			
17. Progressive Maturation in the Christian Life	9–12			
18. Making Love a Priority in Living	13			
TOTAL				

Initiatives for Moving from Pew to Pavement

Pray for one another, so that you may be healed.
(James 5:16)

Godly reconciliation calls for us to focus on and communicate with God in order to gain the inner strength and supernatural wisdom we need in these times. We must use all kinds of prayers in all kinds of venues.

ACTIVITIES

Goal: Covenant to pray personally and increasingly for your family, your neighborhood, your nation, and every other country in the world (intercessory prayer).

Scripture: John 17:1–26; 1 Timothy 2:1–7

Question: It seems easy to pray for those close to you—for those you love. For whom have you prayed today whom you find it difficult to love? Will you commit to pray for that person (or those persons) until God fills your heart with love for them?

Goal: Examine your motivations for prayer. Do you pray just for "me—myself—mine"? Your soul and spirit should also cry out for the hurts and needs of others. Pray as Jesus prayed.

Scripture: Exodus 34:9; Matthew 6:9–15; James 4:3

Question: When you pray, for what do you pray? For what should you pray?

Goal: Link up with various kinds of groups—prayer meetings, prayer chains, prayer hotlines, prayer walks, and the like—pray alone and pray with others.

Scripture: Matthew 18:19–20; Philippians 4:6

Fill in the blank: _____ can be accomplished through intercessory prayer.

Goal: Encourage your children, youth, and young adults to pray everywhere—including their schools and colleges.

Scripture: Acts 16:13–14; 1 Timothy 2:8

Question: Are there places where you feel uncomfortable praying? Why? How can you overcome this?

Goal: Maintain a "book" of prayers and record the answers.

Scripture: Psalm 25—use the book of Psalms as an example.

Question: What does Psalm 25 teach us about David's prayers?

Action: In your daily book of prayers, see if you can answer the following questions:

• What was significant about what I studied in God's Word?

• How did God specifically answer prayer?

• What happened in spiritual warfare?

• Overall, what did God teach me?

Now by this we may be sure that we know him,
if we obey his commandments.
(1 JOHN 2:3)

We cannot be effective peacemakers if we have not been reconciled to God through faith in Jesus Christ. To "do" reconciliation, we must "think" reconciliation, which means "thinking" God's thoughts.

ACTIVITIES

Goal: Be sure that you are reconciled by repenting of anything that cuts you off from right relationship with God or other people.

Scripture: Proverbs 15:8, 29; Ezekiel 14:6; Luke 18:9–14; 1 John 1:8–10

Question: As you regularly ask God to show you your sin and help you repent of it, how does this prepare you to face future temptation?

Goal: Examine yourself to see if you are obeying the Great Commandment to love God with all your heart, soul, mind, and strength and your neighbor as yourself.

Scripture: Luke 10:25–29

Action: Pray for help to love God with all your heart, mind, strength, and to love your neighbors as yourself—more and more each day. Ask God to show you your neighbors.

Goal: Initiate reconciling action now with someone from whom you have been estranged. Learn from Jesus how to forgive.

Scripture: Matthew 5:21–24; Luke 23:34

Fill in the blank: I have quarreled with _____.
Before I pray for my own needs or go to sleep tonight, I need to _____ to reconcile or begin the reconciliation process for this relationship.

Goal: Examine yourself to see how your attitude may have contributed to divisiveness anywhere.

Scripture: Matthew 7:1–5; Mark 9:50; 1 Thessalonians 5:11,14

Action: Take intentional action to be a peacemaker now (or as soon as possible).

Question: How do your personal actions affect your witness for God? How do your actions glorify God?

FAMILY INITIATIVE

Every city or house divided against itself shall not stand.
(MATTHEW 12:25, KJV)

"Charity (love) begins at home" is an old but true saying. The same thing is true about reconciliation. Our homes should be prime examples of peaceful, joyous living.

ACTIVITIES

Goal: Purposefully initiate sincere efforts to restore communication, settle differences, and revive unconditional love between yourself and all family members, especially those from whom you are estranged.

Scripture: Matthew 5:21–24; Mark 3:23–35

Question: How many families do you know of that try to reconcile their differences? How many families do you know who don't try to reconcile their differences? What is the difference in the results?

Goal: Examine yourself to see how you may have contributed to any division in your family and be willing to repent. Learn from Jesus how to love.

Scripture: Mark 1:40–42; John 15:13

Question: Who in your family is difficult to love? Perhaps they are quarrelsome. Perhaps they have a frightening disease. Perhaps they do not act like you or smell right. Are you willing to go to them and walk with them and hold their hand and talk to them as they seek out the truth of the love of God, which you are seeking as well? How will you do this?

Goal: Let go of bitterness, embrace forgiveness, and continually learn to pray and have fun together. Your forgiveness could unlock someone's repentance.

Scripture: John 4:5–42

Question: How does Jesus react to the Samaritan woman? How would you have reacted? What types of people today are treated like the Samaritan woman? Minorities? Homosexuals? Feminists? AIDS patients? Politicians? Slumlords? Drug abusers? How will you react to these people in the future?

CHURCH INITIATIVE

*For the time has come for judgment to begin
with the household of God.*
(1 PETER 4:17)

$\mathbf{T}$he church—the household of God—is made up of those persons who believe that God is the only creator and supreme ruler of the universe and that Jesus Christ is God's Son and our Savior.

ACTIVITIES

Goal: Plan/participate in a prayer vigil at your place of worship.

Scripture: Acts 12:5–11; 27:23–25; Colossians 4:2,3

Fill in the blank: I am going to_____ in the prayer vigil.

Goal: Take deliberate action to reach out to a fellowship of believers whose label differs from yours. Do not wait for a group to come to you—you go to them. Sponsor joint worship and Bible study, and be a witness.

Scripture: Matthew 28:19–20; Acts 8:26–35

Question: How can you listen to God's nudgings (like Philip) and reach out to others who aren't in your circles of influence?

Goal: Make room for all the gifts of all the people in your fellowship.

Scripture: Joel 2:28; Mark 12:41–44; Romans 12:4–8

Question: Have you discounted the gift of a brother or sister because it's too small, ordinary, "not in my ministry," or too difficult to identify? How will you work to include these people?

Goal: Pastors can plan "pulpit exchanges," particularly across denominational, racial, and cultural lines. Proclaim the message of reconciliation.

Scripture: Acts 11:19–26; 1 Corinthians 3:9

Question: Paul continually meets with and writes to different congregations. In what ways will your congregation work with another congregation?

- In your city? _____
- In another part of your country? _____
- In another language/cultural background? _____
- In another country? _____

Goal: Plan for times of united fellowships, gatherings, witnessing, or community projects. You will learn something good and you will be blessed.

Scripture: Acts 2:42; Ephesians 2:19; James 2:1–7

Question: When planning gatherings and fellowship times, whom will you invite?

Goal: As a group, commit to sustain the action(s) initiated at this time.

Scripture: James 5:12,16

Question: What specific actions will you commit to sustain at this time? How can you leave room for growth?

BUSINESS/POLITICAL/ NATIONAL/INTERNATIONAL INITIATIVE

He that ruleth over men must be just, ruling in the fear of God.
(2 SAMUEL 23:3, KJV)

The most important consideration in these arenas must be the recognition that all authority comes ultimately from the omnipotent God. *"In him we live and move and have our being"* (Acts 17:28). *"He changes times and seasons, deposes kings and sets up kings; he gives wisdom to the wise"* (Daniel 2:21). *"What does the Lord require of you but to do justice, and to love kindness, and to walk humbly with your God?"* (Micah 6:8). The Bible teaches that it is the responsibility of the strong to help the weak.

ACTIVITIES

Goal: Recognize that human power and place in leadership will continue only as long as God and the people allow it. *"Every good and perfect gift is from above"* (James 1:17, NIV).

Scripture: 1 Samuel 10:7–11, 15; John 19:10–11

Question: How do you treat those over whom you have authority, and how do you respond to those who have power over you—if they are just? if they are unjust? How should you respond?

Goal: Examine diligently and, if necessary, amend laws and policies making sure that they are just for *all people* in your business, electorate, state, or nation. Remember that reparation is often an ingredient of reconciliation. Read the story of Jesus' encounter with Zacchaeus—Luke 19:1–10.

Scripture: Habakkuk 2:2–17

Question: How will you work to create laws, policies, or programs promoting social justice? Since the process is usually slow, what will you do *now* to be an example of God's passion for social justice?

Goal: Ask God to help you to change habits that are divisive, disruptive, or discourteous.

Scripture: Matthew 7:12

Question: Do you do things to others that you do not like people to do to you? I.e., Do you interrupt? Do you ignore? Do you insult? Do you belittle? How do you share with others?

Goal: Learn from Jesus the Messiah how to serve.

Scripture: Matthew 12:18–21; 15:21–28; 20:25–28; 27:27–54; John 13:3–5

Question: The Canaanite woman (Matthew 15:21–28) only asked for the crumbs of the life Jesus was offering to the Jews—crumbs that would heal her daughter! If it takes only crumbs of faith to heal a person, how much can your crumbs of faith do to bring reconciliation in any relationship? Do you have faith in your own crumbs of faithful service?

RACIAL/CULTURAL/COMMUNITY INITIATIVE

*There is no longer Jew or Greek, there is no longer
slave or free, there is no longer male and female;
for all of you are one in Christ Jesus.*
(GALATIANS 3:28)

Reconcilers must get rid of the attitudinal lenses (how we see other people) that color our perspectives, create our stereotypes, promote our prejudices, and dictate our discriminatory actions.

ACTIVITIES

Goal: Make a decision now to "see" every other person as God sees them—made in God's image and worth more than the whole world. Intentionally and prayerfully begin to establish one-to-one reconciling relationships—now!

Scripture: Genesis 1:27, 31; 5:1–2; Matthew 5:43–48

Fill in the blank: I will try to look at _____ as a child of God, even though s/he is hard to love. I will forgive _____ even if s/he will not express repentance or ask for forgiveness—even if s/he does not realize what s/he is doing.

Goal: Acknowledge that problems of estrangement exist and have damaging effects on individuals and society. Be aware that neutrality can perpetuate evil.

Scripture: Romans 12:10,21; Philippians 2:3

Question: In what ways and about which issues are you "lukewarm"?

Goal: Examine yourself to see if you have belittled any person of any gender, race, color, class, creed, or religious persuasion. Any such action, whether done openly or secretly, is an act of violence and should not be continued. Often the things that bother us most about others are things that are true about us. Examine yourself and your judgments. If you find the same sin in your life as you find in another, repent of your own sin first—then it is easier to go with a loving and gracious heart to your brother or sister who exhibits the same sin, since you know the sacrifice of repentance.

Scripture: Luke 6:39–42; Colossians 3:8–17

Fill in the blank: As a child of God, I need to work with my brothers and sisters in Christ to _____ in order to be right with God.

Goal: Take responsibility *now* for reducing polarization rather than blaming others for it. Learn from Jesus how to be a peacemaker.

Scripture: Luke 10:2–6; Acts 11:1–19

Question: How has Jesus asked us to be peacemakers?

Goal: Recognize that reconciliation always includes a cycle of repentance and forgiveness for the persons and groups involved. With God's empowerment, reconciliation is always possible though Jesus, the Prince of Peace.

Scripture: Matthew 18:21–22; Luke 6:35; Colossians 3:15

Question: What is the biblical cycle of repentance and forgiveness? Look at Old Testament as well as New Testament examples.

Goal: Focus on the similarities between human beings—this will be an eye-opening challenge to your perceived dissimilarities.

Scripture: John 10:16; Galatians 3:27–29; Ephesians 1:10; 2:14

Question: What are some similarities between human beings that surprise you?

Goal: Be aware that reconciliation is the work of God and must be based on the building of personal relationships before it can be effective programmatically.

Scripture: Ephesians 2:11–22; Matthew 5:23–26

Question: What are some dangers of programmatic reconciliation that bypass the building of relationships?

Goal: Leaders of reconciling ministries and groups should plan "together" sessions centered around coordination of their efforts.

Scripture: Acts 11:19–20; 14:27–28

Question: What kind of groups do you know that would benefit from coordination of their efforts with your group or other groups? How can you help them?

MEDIA INITIATIVE

Whatever is true, whatever is noble, whatever is right,
whatever is pure, whatever is lovely, whatever is
admirable—if anything is excellent or praiseworthy—
think about [and spread] such things.
(PHILIPPIANS 4:8, NIV)

High-tech communication systems and all of their accessories have brought just about every proclaimer of every theory and ideology into our homes. As the distance between people and ideas becomes increasingly narrower, the battle for the domination of human minds rages between the controllers and distributors of every kind of communication. It is critical that media owners, mangers, producers, distributors and consumers understand and take part in the responsibility for uniting diverse cultures as we continue to uphold our First Amendment rights.

ACTIVITIES

Goal: Seek to build up and maintain godly moral and ethical values in the society.

Scripture: 1 Corinthians 1:25; James 3:13–18

Question: How can you help to build up and maintain godly moral and ethical values in our society today?

Goal: Develop major media presentations that foster cohesiveness among people of all languages, races, colors, cultures, genders, and classes.

Scripture: 2 Timothy 2:20–26

Question: How might you promote media presentations that foster cohesiveness among all people yet are also exciting or intriguing enough for the media companies to accept and put forth?

Goal: Use communication skills to build understanding, minimize fragmentation, and stop proliferation of divisively slanted news among polarized groups.

Scripture: Acts 10:28; 1 Timothy 1:4–7

Question: How do you, in your daily walk, work to build understanding, minimize fragmentation, and stop proliferation of divisively slanted news among polarized groups? Are there other ways you can work at this?

Goal: Continually seek to eliminate the depiction of (physical/mental/emotional) violence and indecency as being normal behavior.

Scripture: 2 Timothy 3:1–9

Question: Have you ever been exposed to belittlement or physical, emotional, or sexual violence? What kinds of attitudes do you still maintain about these? What kind of violent behavior have you initiated? How can you become involved in reconciling action with people who are abusive?

Goal: Make intentional efforts to uncover the presuppositions of all who claim to describe the truth of any matter.

Scripture: 1 Corinthians 3:18–20; 2 Timothy 6:20

Question: As you hold onto the truth of Jesus, how can you help others who stray from the truth of Jesus?

Goal: Consider the validity of objective truth and universal principle to be, at least, possible.

Scripture: John 1:1–5; Acts 4:10–12

Action: Ask for wisdom from the Creator of the universe to help you to understand how to interact with those who need to be liberated so that they can express love to people around them.

The Basis of Godly, Holistic Reconciliation: Building Relationships in All Areas of Living

"God **reconciled** us to himself through Jesus Christ"

"Christ has given us the ministry of **reconciliation**"

"He has committed to us the ministry of **reconciliation**"

"We implore you . . . be **reconciled** to God"

FAMILY MEMBERS
(Spouses, parents, children, in-laws, extended family members)

CLERGY—IN ALL CHURCHES, TEMPLES, MOSQUES, & SYNAGOGUES
(The leaders must lead in the reconciling process)

CHURCH LEADERS AT ALL LEVELS
(Officers within each fellowship)

CHRISTIAN BUSINESS PEOPLE
(Owners/managers, through all levels of staff)

COMMUNITY RESIDENTS
(Be in touch with persons—problems, strengths in each area)

CROSS-GENERATIONAL GROUPS
(Young, middle-aged, seniors)

CONGREGATIONS AS A WHOLE & AMONG INDIVIDUAL MEMBERS
(Interdenominational and intra-church linkages)

COMMUNITY AGENCIES—INCLUD-ING GOVERNMENTAL, NONPROFIT & PARACHURCH GROUPS
(Efforts must be made not to "reinvent the wheel")

GOVERNMENTAL/POLITICAL GROUPS
(All parties and factions)

INTERRACIAL AND CROSS-CULTURAL GROUPS
(National and traditional languages/values/concerns must be openly acknowledged and addressed)

The people of God must intentionally build relationships with each of these persons and groups. The lasting effects of reconciliation are directly related to the one-on-one relationships that are developed and nurtured within and among these groups.

A Kaleidoscopic Picture
of Reconciliation

Reconciliation Is God's Agenda

LOUIS AND COLLEEN EVANS

RECONCILIATION IS GOD'S AGENDA! JESUS SECURED THAT AGENDA WHEN HE went to the cross. If you and I have been reconciled to God in Christ, then we are called to follow the example of Jesus and to continue his work of reconciliation in the world. Quite simply, we do the work of God by being the people of God. No one we have ever known has been more passionately dedicated to this truth in principle or more effective in living it out than Sam Hines. This we know because our lives have been forever blessed since entering into a covenant relationship over twenty years ago with Sam and Dalineta (Vickie) Hines. They, along with John and Pauline (Vivian) Staggers, shared with us their vision of Washington, D.C., as a city on a hill for God. We often prayed that together we would be a model of love and reconciliation. Our two congregations joined in ministry to the hungry and homeless of our city. On occasion, we worshiped and "retreated" together. But to be honest, more than the vision and partnership in ministry, it was the relationship we shared with this brother and sister in Christ that touched us at the deepest level. It was real. Although Sam has left us physically, the covenant continues.

Sam believed that God created diversity—diversity of race, culture, personality, and appearance—not by chance, but by design. He did not see diversity as an obstacle to overcome, but an opportunity to be a part of God's good plan. Out of that conviction Sam had the most incredible ability to help people from every conceivable background—the powerful and the powerless—move beyond their alienation and polarization, even beyond accepting one another in their diversity, to a new place where they embraced and invited one another into their lives and ever-expanding circles of love. Sam and Vickie did this for us, and we never will be the same. Sam not only "talked the talk," but "walked the walk," in his own personal journey, within his rich family life, and in his powerful prophetic ministry to Third Street Church of God and to the world.

Louis Evans served for many years as the senior pastor of the National Presbyterian Church in Washington, D.C. He and his wife, noted author Colleen Evans, were covenant partners with Samuel and Dalineta Hines.

Farewell to Sam Hines

But Not to His Message and Ministry

SETHARD BEVERLY

Sam, my dear friend and brother, died very suddenly and without warning. While working through the grief and reality of Sam's death, I processed who Sam was and the impact he made on my life, the church, and society at large. That he was no "ordinary" fellow is evidenced by the thousands of people who attended his funeral—from all over the nation, as well as from outside the United States and Canada. And everyone felt close to Sam. He had a big heart. We all miss Sam's presence, his personality, wit, preaching, and that boisterous laugh of his. But two things we need not miss about this larger-than-life saint are his message of reconciliation and ministry of inclusiveness. He lived both and left many memories and audiotapes that all of us will revisit often for the rest of our lives. God did a special thing in Sam Hines.

Sam's Reconciliation Ministry and Message

Sam realized very early in his life how essential the message of reconciliation is to this conflict-driven, polarized world—and how pervasive the Bible is in its insistence that reconciliation is the heart of God's eternal purpose for humankind in Jesus Christ. Sam saw that what the world needs at every level (family, church, community, class, ethnic groups, nations) is the reconciliation that God effects in Christ, both vertically and horizontally, and he lived out this message. Very often in my dealings with Sam the only cause to which I could attribute his conclusions or actions was his strong commitment to reconciliation. Today we sometimes hear evangelicals talking about reconciliation, but if we could trace this movement back to its source, we would likely be led to Dr. Samuel G. Hines, who began expounding and disseminating the neglected message in the 1960s. A check of evangelical publications before that time will corroborate this. Even when Christian unity was being discussed, reconciliation often went unmentioned.

Sam's Inclusive Ministry

The international/interdenominational church held Sam in high esteem for his brilliant expository preaching. Added to that was his global Christian statesmanship, which extended to Europe, Asia, and the West Indies, and to South Africa during the years of apartheid, where he was involved in discussions with political and church leaders from all tribes and groups regarding the need to forgive and be reconciled to one another in Christ. Sam practiced what he preached, in the abstract and in the concrete. In fact, the best "picture" I have of Sam is not of him preaching at conventions or presiding over the Church of God's General Assembly. My most treasured image of Sam Hines comes out of the daily Urban Prayer Breakfast, where his church fed, evangelized, discipled, and mentored several hundred homeless people five days a week for more than fifteen years. Sam had just concluded his homily when he called for those who wanted prayer to move forward. A dozen or so persons came, many of them dirty and smelly. But that did not disturb Sam. No, no. He simply reached out his arms and drew as many as he could to himself, hugging them while he prayed for them to accept God's love. When I saw that, something within me shouted, "Now that's the spirit of Jesus!"

See you later, Sam.

P.S. On the morning that Samuel Hines died (in a Washington, D.C., hospital), his eldest son, David, was proclaiming the Word at that Urban Prayer Breakfast in the church—that ministry still continues to transform lives.

Sethard Beverly retired from many years of service in the Church of God (Anderson, Ind.) as the director of Metro Urban Ministries and as a pastor. He was a close friend of Samuel Hines. This epilogue was originally published as Sethard Beverly, "Farewell to Sam Hines, but Not to His Message and Ministry," *Metro-Voice,* Winter 1994–95, 1.